Taking the Stress Out of Bad Behaviour

Also available from Continuum

101 Essential Lists for Managing Behaviour in the Early Years,
Simon Brownhill, Clare Gratton and Fiona Shelton

Managing Behaviour in the Early Years, Janet Kay

Managing Your Classroom, second edition, Gererd Dixie

Taking the Stress Out of Bad Behaviour

Behaviour Management of 3–11 year olds

SIMON BROWNHILL

continuum

Continuum International Publishing Group
The Tower Building, 11 York Road, London, SE1 7NX
80 Maiden Lane, Suite 704, New York, NY 10038

www.continuumbooks.com

British Library Cataloguing-in-Publication Data
A catalogue record for this book is available from the British Library.

ISBN: 0–8264–9563–X (paperback)

Library of Congress Cataloging-in-Publication Data
Brownhill, Simon.
    Taking the stress out of bad behaviour : behaviour management of 3–11 year olds / Simon Brownhill.
        p. cm.
    Includes index.
    ISBN-13: 978–0–8264–9563–1 (pbk.)
    ISBN-10: 0–8264–9563–X (pbk.)
    1. Behavior modification--Great Britain. 2. Problem children--Education--Great Britain. 3. Classroom management--Great Britain. I. Title.

    LB1060.2.B76 2007
    371.39′3--dc22

                                                            2007017767

Illustrations by Kerry Ingham
Designed and typeset by Kenneth Burnley, Wirral, Cheshire
Printed and bound in Great Britain by Antony Rowe Ltd, Chippenham, Wiltshire

To Fiona and the Groovy Gang,
both young and old(er)

Contents

Acknowledgements

Without the support, ideas, advice and guidance given by the following people this book would not have been written:

Christina Garbutt, Commissioning Editor at Continuum Publishing, for taking a second gamble and allowing me to 'go it alone' this time around, and Ruth Stimson for her rigorous timetable and planning.

Dr Des Hewitt at the University of Derby who gave me the original idea for this book via comments he made relating to my first collaborative book on behaviour management. Des, you said that the book 'worked best when the lists were specific to a particular behaviour'. Well, here's a book full of them. Does it still work?

All the practitioners (those training, with NQT status or experienced) I have spoken to who generously gave their time to suggest behaviours which could be explored in this book, especially Angela Whittle and members of the BEd Year One cohort (2005–6).

Irene Woodward for allowing me to tap into her wealth of teaching experience.

Fiona Shelton, my top friend and initial editor – thanks for the 'aged' behaviours in Chapter 1! Massive thanks must also go to Karen and Kelly Fisher for extensively supporting the editing process along with the Teaching Assistants on the Foundation Degree Behaviour Management module (2006–7).

My fantastic family, superb second family, wealth of wonderful friends and the brilliant colleagues and students I have the pleasure of working with at the University of Derby.

Many thanks must go to the children who were used in the photographs in this book and their parents/carers who gave permission for the photographs to be taken. Thank you to Richard Richards at the university for taking the pictures for me and for Chris Seabridge for agreeing to be photographed at short notice! *I would like to make it clear that the behaviours exhibited by the children in these images bear absolutely no resemblance to the real behaviours or academic capabilities of those captured in these photographs.*

Finally, a thank you must go to the reader – most people never actually read the acknowledgements! Thank you for believing this book will make a positive impact on your practice – I promise you it will!
Thank you all very much.

SPB

Terminology clarification

For the purposes of clarification the following terms and their specific meanings are used throughout this book:

Practitioner meaning any adult who works with children in an educational setting.

School meaning any setting where children may access the six areas of learning in the Early Years Foundation Stage from 36 months upwards and the subject areas which form the National Curriculum for Key Stages 1 and 2.

Classroom meaning any space in which children are taught.

Icons

Question mark – This indicates parts of the text where you should take time out and think about the issues raised in relation to your own practice or experiences.

Case Study – This highlights real-life examples of practice that you can either emulate or avoid!

Scenario – This provides imagined situations that allow you to select different strategies for managing a particular behaviour, so you can think about putting the theory into practice.

Exclamation Mark – This details important points to help you gain perspective on behavioural difficulties; they represent a reality check.

Activity – This gives you the opportunity to engage with a quick task – you might want a pen and paper handy!

Top Tip – These are useful pieces of advice that you might want to try out.

Introduction

Effective behaviour management holds the key to successful learning and teaching. As a result, all practitioners are keen to develop strategies, techniques and approaches to manage children's behaviour so that it does not interfere with the quality of teaching provision in the classroom.

This book has been developed to specifically support practitioners working with children between the ages of three (36 months) and eleven, and is designed to help manage behaviours which practitioners *want* and *have* to be able to manage effectively on a day-to-day basis. To put each of these behaviours into a real-life context 'on the shop floor', each behavioural issue is introduced by a practitioner who personally would like to manage it or manage it better!

It is important to remember that there is no 'quick fix' in terms of managing children's behaviour in the classroom. While the wealth of positive strategies, ideas and top tips on offer in this book may make the reader believe they have 'all they need' to cope with behavioural issues in their classroom, readers should note that behaviour management is a long and challenging journey, and what may work with one group of children may be totally ineffective in managing the behaviour of others. With this in mind readers are reminded to select, adapt and implement strategies they feel will be effective in their classroom with their children, and that these should be used regularly and consistently to have the maximum effect.

This book has been written to purposefully develop critical thinking and reflection in those who actively engage with it. Throughout the book readers will find a number of case studies, scenarios, practical activities and reflective questions and tasks with which to engage. These are designed to allow the reader to make professional judgements and decisions about behaviour management on a short-, medium- and long-term basis, challenging thinking and reflecting critically on current practice, while adapting, modifying and introducing new knowledge, skills and understanding in order to 'take the stress out of bad behaviour'.

This book has just one aim: to promote good behaviour in children and discourage poor behaviour. It is up to the reader to determine whether this book successfully achieves its aim.

1 | Typical behaviours across the age phases

1. Three years old and using the word 'No!'

We have just had the new intake in the nursery and one little girl has been immediately spotted by the team as being 'oppositional'. No matter what request we ask of her she flatly refuses to comply, shouting 'No!' at the top of her voice and then quickly folds her arms, crouching down on the floor with her head held low. She will stay like this for the rest of the session – if we try to move her she screams out loud: 'NO! NO! NO! NO! NO!' Any ideas on why she is doing this?

Nursery practitioner

Point to note: While it is inevitable for practitioners to talk to one another about the behaviours they see in school, it is important to avoid labelling children with names, terms and phrases as they have the potential to 'stick' in people's minds long after the behaviour has been effectively managed.

Clearly there is a problem and practitioners need to collaborate together to determine:

A   Why the child is behaving in the way that they are
B   What strategies they can put in place to manage this behaviour.

What do you think about A and B?

Take a moment to consider your thoughts, feelings and ideas relating to the points identified above. Use the table overleaf to record your thinking.

Why might the child be behaving in this way?	What strategies could be put in place to support the child and thus manage her behaviour?

Read the rest of this section and then reflect on your initial ideas – does it support, extend or challenge your thinking?

For any child entering an Early Years Foundation Stage setting (Nursery particularly) it can be an unsettling time for a number of reasons. These include:

◆ being away from their main carer for a period of time;
◆ being expected to stay in a strange environment until their main carer collects them;
◆ working with adults whom they do not know;
◆ being expected to play with other children whom they have never met before;
◆ understanding and following rules and routines which are different from those at home;
◆ not having any home comforts around them, e.g. their own teddy bear, their own toilet, their own toys etc.

Most practitioners are aware that children (and carers) will experience some or all of these concerns and will have in place appropriate policies, induction programmes and practical strategies to make children's first few weeks in nursery as stress-free and as enjoyable as possible.

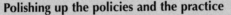

Polishing up the policies and the practice

Spend some time with your colleagues looking through policies, procedures and practice you adopt to induct new children into the setting. Consider ways in which you can improve on your practice to date. Discuss these ideas with your head-teacher, other settings and local authority advisers.

While the above is a positive thing to do it may not actually help us to effectively manage the behaviour detailed at the start of this section: 'No! No! No!' Let's consider the reasoning as to why the child may be doing this:

◆ attention seeking;
◆ issues at home;
◆ child thinks it is a game;
◆ lack of understanding of the social organization of the setting;
◆ tiredness or exhaustion;
◆ feeling poorly;
◆ personality trait – stubbornness;
◆ child is trying to 'establish themselves' in the setting.

Management strategies to deal with this behaviour need to not only support the child but also make it clear that this behaviour is not acceptable in the setting.
  Please do:

◆ calmly ask the child what is wrong;
◆ empathize with the child – make them appreciate that you know how they feel;
◆ leave the child alone for a while – they may do as you ask later on;
◆ assess whether your requests are reasonable;

- offer some form of comfort – a teddy to cuddle, a little hug to support them emotionally;
- talk through issues with the child;
- ask parents/carers why they think the child is behaving like this – are they doing the same sort of thing at home?
- give the child some time out;
- pre-warn the child of any changes in the setting before they actually occur;
- remind the child of the rules of the setting.

Please avoid:

- shouting at the child;
- using unnecessary force to physically move the child;
- lecturing the child;
- telling the child off in front of their peers;
- laughing at their emotional outburst.

2. Four years old and being just *too* eager to please

I really enjoy working with Reception children because they are just so keen to learn and be involved in everything! I do have a few problems though with one or two of the children who are just too eager to please me and waste valuable learning and teaching time doing little jobs when they should be working. How can I manage this rather lovely yet irritating behaviour?

Reception practitioner

Most young children are keen to seek praise from virtually anyone, be it practitioners, their parents/carers or their peers. Everyone responds to verbal, non-verbal or written praise irrespective of their age – although we become more embarrassed having it bestowed on us as we get older (even though secretly it gives our self-esteem a serious boost!). Young children particularly relish the feelings associated with receiving praise from others as it helps them to feel loved, appreciated, wanted and valued.

Most children are quick to realize that doing something 'right' or 'good' is an easy way for them to receive praise, particularly if it is noticed by adults around them. There are many ways in which children can please adults e.g. by tidying up or helping to set out resources on the tables.

Reflective Questions

◆ When was the last time you praised a child?
◆ How did you share the praise with the child? Was it verbal, non-verbal or in written form? Why did you choose to share it with them in this way?
◆ How did the child react to the praise? How do you know?
◆ What implicit messages were you passing to the child with your praise? Consider the suggestions provided in the final paragraph prior to this task box.

Take just a moment!

Consider five ways in which children could easily seek praise from you by doing something 'right' or 'good'. Reflect on whether the same children do these things in your class or whether every child has the opportunity to seek this praise from you.

However, some children try a little too hard to please and this can become a real issue if it is not managed effectively. Children who are too eager to please do it for a number of reasons:

◆ child has low self-esteem;
◆ child is attention seeking;
◆ stages of child development – child is still seeking security;
◆ child wants genuine approval;
◆ child is trying to avoid going out to play;
◆ child wants to feel loved;
◆ doing extra jobs gives the child self-importance;
◆ learned behaviour – child has to do jobs at home;
◆ child is lazy – work avoidance tactic;
◆ child does not understand what they have to do and is too frightened to ask for help.

With this in mind practitioners should be aware of the potential issues this behaviour brings into the classroom:

◆ child spends more time pleasing others rather than doing anything of real educational value;
◆ potential issues of favouritism (noted by the other children);
◆ practitioners become irritated by the behaviour;
◆ other children become dependent on one child to 'do' for them;
◆ lots of time wastage;
◆ child begins to sense that helpfulness is not an admired quality – becomes resentful;
◆ child feels disheartened when they are told off.

Top Tip!

Please avoid telling children off for being too helpful – they were, after all, only trying to help! Make them aware that they have done more than their fair share and that they need to ensure everyone else 'pulls their weight'.

With this in mind we now need to consider effective ways to manage this behaviour:

◆ only allow the child to do one key job;
◆ establish class jobs and work these out on a rota every week;
◆ avoid children 'carrying others' in terms of workload;
◆ praise children for their efforts but remind them of the need for quality and not quantity;
◆ ensure your focus is more on children and their work as opposed to jobs they do;
◆ closely observe children when they undertake unnecessary jobs – are they avoiding doing something?
◆ use other practitioners, parent helpers and/or students to tidy up the classroom when you are doing whole class teaching;
◆ issue sanctions to children if they do not respond to your requests;
◆ speak to parents and carers about your concerns – are there patterns in their behaviour at home?

3. Five years old and using 'naughty' words

I'm not sure what has caused it but a number of children in my class have begun to use 'naughty' words in their everyday conversations. They seem to use them to describe each other – 'You're a silly willy!' – and to make each other laugh yet the number of times I have had children crying because they have been called 'bum face' is crazy! How do I even attempt to manage this one?

Year 1 teacher

'Naughty' words? Whatever does he mean?

By the term 'naughty' words we are referring to rude words, two of which are mentioned in the quote above. Without recording some of the more offensive examples (swear words) make a note of words you hear children use in class and on the playground which you would class as 'naughty' or 'rude':

_____

_____

_____

While practitioners, parents and carers try to protect children from bad or inappropriate language, it is inevitable that children will learn and use 'naughty' words for a number of reasons:

1. Peers and siblings will teach children these words either at home or at school (on the playground).
2. Young children think that knowing and using them makes them appear 'grown up'.
3. Children love to learn new words and phrases – most are fascinated by language.
4. Children will hear words and phrases being used on the radio, TV and other types of media.
5. Parents and carers may use them accidentally.
6. These words make other children laugh – humour is a very powerful way to make and keep friends.
7. These words can be used to verbally harm or label others as an act of self-defence if a child is involved in an argument.

Most children like 'naughty' words, and although some children are more reserved in actually using them in conversations, the simple fact of knowing them is enough for them to have a giggle when they hear them being said by others. Children at this age are becoming more aware of their bodies and are particularly fascinated with words which refer to their genitalia and features that differ between the sexes. It is interesting to point out that some children might actually not know what these words mean yet will see others laughing and therefore will join in with the 'joke'.

Children who use these words are:

a) trying to make friends with others by making them laugh;
b) being silly and immature – having a 'childish' moment;
c) trying to deliberately aggravate others – get some sort of response out of them (be it positive or negative);
d) seeking attention;
e) unaware of the meaning of these words.

Scenario

It is 09.03 and you have just brought your class in from the playground. As you settle the children you hear a child in the cloakroom saying to others that they have a 'big botty'. Giggling and loud laughter is heard until one child rushes into the classroom, clearly upset by what has been said about them. What would you do? Record your ideas in the space below.

_____

_____

_____

_____

_____

_____

Compare your ideas to the strategies presented opposite to effectively manage this behaviour.

Clearly this behaviour has the potential to offend others and make children feel uncomfortable or embarrassed about themselves. While children are more likely to use these words in the playground, it is inevitable that they will also be used in class. Practitioners need strategies to hand to manage situations in which these words are used. Suggestions include:

◆ strategically ignore it;
◆ use your 'practitioner glare' to warn children;
◆ speak to the child one-to-one;
◆ use Personal, Health, Social and Citizenship Education (PHSCE) and circle time opportunities to discuss issues which are as a result of children using 'naughty' words;
◆ clearly state that you do not want to hear language like that in your classroom again;
◆ talk to the class about appropriate and inappropriate forms of language;
◆ laugh with the children – 'bottom' *is* a funny word!
◆ talk about what these words actually mean and refer to – is it funny now?
◆ use role play and other drama conventions to explore thoughts and feelings of others who have to listen to language like this;
◆ read and discuss stories (in book or verbal form) which involve children using 'naughty' words;
◆ talk about the qualities of a good child – is using 'naughty' words in public a good quality or not?
◆ use your class rules to remind children about how they are not to use 'naughty' words.

4. Six years old and learning how to hurt the feelings of others

I'm not too sure why but the children in my class seem to take great delight at the moment in saying and doing things to hurt the feelings of their friends and others in their class. The tears and tantrums which result in the comments and actions being made are quite unbelievable – why are they behaving in this way? It is really unpleasant and some of the children do not want to come to school as a result of it.

Year 2 teacher

As most children develop so too does their ability to acquire, manipulate and use language in a variety of contexts for numerous reasons. This language is not solely speech-based; children of this age are very good at reading and using body language to convey thoughts, feelings and ideas.

How do they say it *without* saying a word?

Consider how children might say the following without using words to express themselves:

◆ 'I really like you!'
◆ 'You smell!'
◆ 'Do you want to play with me?'
◆ 'That was so boring!'
◆ 'I'm tired!'
◆ 'I'm really angry because you have just trodden on my foot!'
◆ 'Just leave me alone!'

Reflect on how children may combine facial expressions, hand gestures, body language and sounds to elicit these ideas. Take a moment to consider how your body language in the classroom influences the way in which children respond to you. Ask a colleague to observe your body language during some whole class teaching – how does it have an effect on the children's behaviour in class?

As most children grow in confidence and ability not all of them are able to rely on their physical strength to help them win any arguments or fights they may get themselves into. As a result, many develop an ability to use words, phrases and gestures to pass on messages to others which are specifically designed to emotionally wound others. But we still need to be clear as to why children of this age seem intent on hurting the feelings of others.

A picture says a thousand words! Body language helps practitioners to acknowledge how children are feeling. What do you think the children above are thinking/feeling? Why do you think this?

Why do they do it?

Reflect on an incident in your class when a child has been hurt by the words or actions of others. Consider which of the reasoning below helps to establish why children hurt the feelings of others:

- ◆ They do not actually realize their words/actions hurt others – 'just a bit of fun!'
- ◆ It is a way of seeking attention.
- ◆ They are unhappy with their own life and so want to make someone else's life miserable.
- ◆ It is retaliation against some form of bullying a child has had to endure.
- ◆ Possible jealousy of what another child has got (e.g. iPod) or is (kind, popular).
- ◆ The child is trying to establish themselves as 'top dog' in the class – a way of eliciting power.

Children of this age are notorious for engaging in numerous activities to hurt the feelings of others. These include:

- name calling;
- ignoring friends;
- refusing to play with others;
- breaking off friendships;
- mocking others ('Just look at her shoes!');
- physically hurting others by squeezing, punching or kicking;
- ganging up on one child.

Clearly this behaviour has the potential to harm children both physically and emotionally, and may result in children becoming withdrawn, weepy or not wanting to come to school. With the possibility of academic performance and children's general well-being deteriorating practitioners need to act quickly to ensure this behaviour does not interfere with learning, teaching and children's lives outside of school.

Selecting Strategies

Read through the strategies below and select three which you feel will help you to manage this behaviour as and when it occurs in your classroom:

- Use PHSCE and circle time opportunities to discuss issues relating to this behaviour in the classroom.
- Praise children who are kind and thoughtful to others.
- Look for the good in those who hurt others – make them feel good so they will do the same to others.
- Use stories to explore how words and actions can hurt others.
- Establish sanctions (agreed with the children) relating to what will happen if they deliberately hurt others in the class.
- Read and reflect on the school rules – what should the children be doing on a daily basis?
- Encourage children to talk through their problems with each other.
- Talk to the children about how they would feel if they were on the 'other side' of the words/actions.

5. Seven years old and the formation of 'groovy gangs'

Just recently I have noticed a kind of 'gang culture' developing in my class. The children have formed little friendship groups that seem to do things together. While I do not mind this, I am becoming concerned about the issues which occur when two groups clash with each other. How can I manage these situations?

Year 3 teacher

Reflection Time!

◆ How many friendship groups are you aware of in your class?
◆ Who are the 'leaders' of each group? Who are the 'followers'?
◆ How many children are not in any of these 'gangs'? Why is this the case?
◆ What kind of things do the children do in their little gangs?
◆ What issues have you had to deal with when two or more gangs clash?

During the early years of their education most children form close friendships with one or two of their peers, yet slowly groups of friends begin to form in which children play with each other in the playground and sit with each other at dinner time/on the carpet on a regular basis. While this is a natural progression in social development and relationships issues begin to crop up when:

◆ 'leaders' try to establish themselves in the group;
◆ groups clash with others;
◆ gangs split up and reform with others;
◆ children who are not in a group try to become part of a 'gang';
◆ children leave one group to join another;
◆ groups take it upon themselves to overpower other children (younger or older) which can lead to bullying.

When I was a child . . .

Think back to when you were at school:

◆ Were you in a 'gang' at school?
◆ What was it like to be in a little gang or what was it like to an outsider?
◆ What were the benefits/disadvantages of being in a gang?

Discuss your thoughts with other colleagues in your school or setting.

While there are many benefits to being part of a 'circle of friends' (comradeship, feeling wanted and loved, supportive atmosphere, always have someone to talk to and play with), there are potential issues (previously mentioned) which may interfere with the quality of learning and teaching in the classroom and the general well being of others in the class.

Case Study

A Year 3 teacher found that groups of friends were becoming unnecessarily intolerant of one another. She found if a child from one group answered a question in class incorrectly members of another group would groan in unison and spend the rest of the lesson sneering at the child, laughing and telling them that they were 'stupid'. This rivalry began to seriously affect standards of attainment in class and a number of children were reported by their parents as not wanting to come to school because children in the 'Smelly Wellies' gang were upsetting and bullying them.

Clearly this behaviour cannot be tolerated. Strategies to manage these behaviours are numerous and depend on the context and the severity of the situations which occur:

◆ Use PHSCE and circle time opportunities to discuss the issues relating to friendship groups not getting on with each other.
◆ Discuss issues with the headteacher and the senior management team if appropriate/necessary.
◆ Use collective worship and assembly time to raise awareness of the dangers of gang culture.
◆ Talk to the children about what it should mean to be in a gang. Stress the positive things gangs can do as opposed to the negatives.
◆ Remind children of the rules of the classroom/school.
◆ Challenge children who break the rules.
◆ Display your expectations which relate to being part of a friendship gang.
◆ Design activities which encourage children to work with others in the class, giving them lettered or numbered heads.
◆ Read stories which explore the concept of gangs of children working together and having fun.
◆ Work collaboratively with parents and carers to manage any issues as a result of friendship gangs clashing.
◆ Encourage children to adopt an 'open door' policy to talk about any issues they might have.

Points to note
Most children play very happily together in their own little groups and most of the time they are able to collaborate and work/play with others in their class without much difficulty. It is only when groups begin to take themselves too seriously (think of the musical films *Grease* and *West Side Story*) that issues will develop.

6. Eight years old and coping with criticism

I am finding that children in my class are becoming increasingly 'crushed' by the criticism I give them relating to their work or behaviour. They were usually able to accept it but now I have tears and tantrums and children refusing to do any more work. What can I do about this?

Year 4 teacher

Everybody finds criticism at some time or another hard to accept and manage; it can leave you deflated, unhappy and unmotivated, particularly if the criticism is seemingly harsh or unnecessary. Most children are 'sensitive little souls' and need to feel what they do is commendable and valued. Criticism can really affect children and so it is important for practitioners to take care when they use this with their class.

Questioning criticism

◆ When was the last time you were critical of a child's work or behaviour?
◆ How did you share this criticism – visual, written or verbal means?
◆ How carefully did you think about the criticism before you gave it?
◆ How did the child react?
◆ Was this reaction expected or not?
◆ Could you have shared the criticism in a better way with the child?

Criticism is a valuable way in which people can grow and develop in terms of their capabilities and approaches to working and living. While many feel disheartened upon finding out they have done something wrong/badly, there are others who see criticism as a way of helping them to move forwards, and react positively to it, spurring them on to try harder and show others they can improve. This can only be achieved if the criticism is constructive in nature.

Find Out!

What do you already know about constructive criticism? How does it work and how can/do you use it with children in the classroom? Take a few moments to look at the following website to develop your knowledge and practice:
http://adhd-add.blogspot.com/2005/04/how-to-give-constructive-criticism.html

So why do some children sometimes respond negatively to criticism? Possible reasons include:

◆ child is unwell or tired;
◆ the work produced is the best they can do at that particular time;
◆ criticism is unnecessarily harsh or delivered in an aggressive tone;
◆ child does not know how to improve their behaviour or work – they need more guidance;
◆ criticism is too personal for the child – undermines their confidence;
◆ child feels the practitioner does not like them if they do not say nice things about them;
◆ criticism lowers the child's self-worth and esteem;
◆ child did not understand the task.

Clearly many emotions are associated with giving and receiving criticism and children need to be taught how to manage these feelings so they do not become potentially depressed by comments made about them or their work.

Case Study

A Year 4 teacher used a variety of learning and teaching strategies to help her class appreciate that giving and receiving criticism is part of everyday life. She used role play scenarios with masks and props, composed songs and even allowed the children to constructively criticize her teaching by playing Mr and Mrs OFSTED!

By seeing the practitioner accept and positively respond to the criticism she was given (apparently she shouted a lot, so began to use a quieter voice), the children quickly began to feel comfortable with giving and receiving criticism from each other.

So, how can we help children cope with criticism? In addition to the ideas above practitioners should ensure they:

◆ think carefully before they say or write something critical;
◆ always start with a positive – adopt the 'two stars and a wish' approach;

◆ speak calmly to the child;
◆ offer ways to improve their work or behaviour – provide a choice so that children feel in control;
◆ set SMART targets;
◆ comment on the work or behaviour and not the child;
◆ empathize with how the child may be feeling.

Top Tip!

Practitioners should remember that everyone responds differently to criticism; some may cry, some may go very quiet for a while, some may want some time on their own and some may bury themselves back into their work. Please avoid trying to engage children in conversation straight after as you will not be their most favourite person at that moment in time!

As a professional if something negative has to be said then it *should* be said. Practitioners should, however, be sensitive to:

a) the way in which this is done;
b) when it is done;
c) whether it should be shared in a private one-to-one or group/class context.

7. Nine/ten years old and a 'sudden stirring of emotions'

Spring has certainly 'sprung' in my class! The children all seem to have caught the 'love bug' and are keen to tell me and each other who they are going out with and who they have just dumped! The problem is that emotions are running rather too high and I constantly seem to be dealing with the distress of the 'dumped'. Any suggestions to help me out with this one?
Year 5 teacher

Up until the age of about eight or nine most girls consider boys to be 'smelly!' while boys regard girls as 'yukky!' There is then a change in the way they regard and look at each other and suddenly everyone is going out with everyone even though some 'relationships' do not actually make it to the end of the first break!

Emotional outbursts!

Reflect on the situation above and identify what strategies you would put in place to manage the children's behaviour, not only at the 'time of the tears' but also after the event when the children have had chance to calm down.

For most children the notion of having a boyfriend or girlfriend is simply a game – they are not really 'going out' with each other; it is more to do with status. These 'couples' may not sit next to each other, talk to each other that much or even play in the same circle of friends, yet their peers are very aware of 'who is going out with whom'.

When a 'relationship' breaks down

Consider the effect a 'break up' could potentially have on learning and teaching in your class. Make a list of issues and consider ways in which you could prevent these issues from escalating into something much worse. An example has been done for you:

Issue	Prevention strategies
Child is too upset to engage with their work.	Have tissues to hand, give the child some time out, allow child to sit next to best friend, encourage child to undertake some deep breathing.

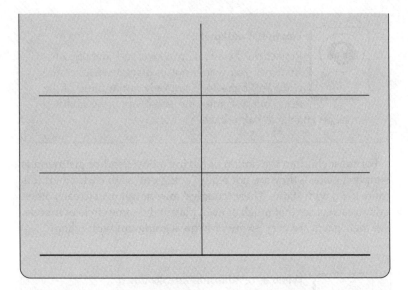

While parents/carers and practitioners will regard boys and girls of this age as still children, many ten year olds consider themselves to be young adults and so having a 'special friend' is one way of indicating their new 'grown up' stage in their life. This thinking is heavily influenced by teenage magazines, soap operas and lyrics to pop songs which may potentially pressurize children into wanting to have a boyfriend or girlfriend.

While most of us recognize that children are quite sensitive, it is unfortunate to report that a child's 'break up' with their 'loved one' can potentially be emotionally upsetting and in some cases will result in a:

◆ lack of sleep and concentration;
◆ loss of appetite resulting in bulimia;
◆ loss of interest in hobbies, friends and life in general;
◆ decline in academic achievement;
◆ an overdose;
◆ self-harming;
◆ attempted suicide.

While you will have identified strategies to manage this behaviour at the time when children are distressed, it is important to put strategies in place to pre-empt relationship-based behaviours.

Do	Avoid
◆ use PHSCE and circle time opportunities to investigate the concept of relationships and what it means to have a boyfriend or girlfriend; ◆ talk about issues relating to emotional well-being during sex education; ◆ teach children to be sensitive to other's feelings; ◆ empathize with children – sometimes love hurts!	◆ telling children they should not have a boyfriend or girlfriend at school; ◆ dictating to children what they should and should not do; ◆ telling children they are 'silly' to feel upset or hurt by the actions of others; ◆ ignoring children who are distressed by matters of the heart.

There are many children, however, who do not fall into the 'good-looking' category and are not considered by their peers as 'worthy companions'. This can have a very adverse effect on a child's self-esteem and self-worth.

Boosting their ego

Take a few moments to look on the internet for three different websites which give guidance, support and strategies to help children who have low self-esteem. Integrate four of these strategies into your practice. Make a note of the date when you started using these strategies:

_____

Review the effectiveness of these strategies in a week's time – have they had a positive impact? If so, what has happened? If not, why have they not worked? Consider the value of using other strategies available.

8. Eleven years old and just 'too cool' for school

I support all the Key Stage 2 classes in school yet find working in Year 6 challenging, particularly in the last term, as the children seem to develop a somewhat unpleasant and lackadaisical attitude to virtually everything linked to being at primary school. How can I work with the class teacher to control the sighing, the sneering and the 'so what' behaviour?

Key Stage 2 teaching assistant

All Year 6 practitioners will notice a change in the way their class conduct and behave themselves in school, particularly after the children have had their SATs tests. Once enthusiastic, hardworking and committed, now the children appear bored, uninterested and rather fed up at having to come to school every day.

Why do you think this is the case?

Make a list of the possible reasons as to why the attitude of the Year 6 children in your school changes during the year. Talk to your Year 6 colleagues to support you if necessary:

◆ _____

◆ _____

◆ _____

◆ _____

◆ _____

Reflect on the strategies suggested below and consider which would be appropriate to respond to the reasons you have identified above.

After many years of being at primary school, children in Year 6 suddenly become the 'top class' and, depending on the way individual schools regard their Year 6 children, with this comes a certain level of responsibility, higher expectations and a status to which the younger children in the school look up.

Questions for reflection

◆ How does your school regard your Year 6 children? Are they seen as 'the oldest children' or as 'young adults'?
◆ Does your school give these children additional responsibilities? If so what are they and how are they given out? If not, why not?
◆ What are the expectations of these children in school? How do the children know what these are?
◆ Do the children recognize they have a powerful status in school? If so, what do they do with this?

While most practitioners consider Year 6 to be in a 'privileged position', most of the children are actually more interested in the imminent move they will make to secondary school. Once the children have experienced 'secondary school life' through various open days and class visits, returning to their primary school is seen by many as being 'babyish', 'old hat' and 'uncool'.

Point to note

Children in Year 6 are really in a difficult transitional point in their lives whereby they are a little too mature in their thinking for primary school, yet are slightly too immature for secondary school. While most children consider themselves ready to take on the challenge of secondary school, practitioners are far more knowing in terms of who could really cope.

It is important for practitioners to recognize the warning signs of when boys' and girls' attitudes towards their primary schooling begin to change as it becomes more difficult to:

◆ motivate and excite the children;
◆ elicit desirable behaviours from them;
◆ keep the children focused on their learning;
◆ prevent younger children modelling the behaviours seen in their 'role models', i.e. their elders.

Activity

How exactly do the behaviours of the Year 6 children 'change'? Consider three different lessons or occasions during the school day and reflect on what behaviours they may model to highlight how 'uncool' they consider being at primary school is. Use the example below to support you:

Assembly/collective worship

Not listening – looking at floor, talking to others.

Not partaking in discussions or answering questions.

Refusing to sing.

Not crossing their legs when sat on the floor.

Embarrassed if asked to come out to the front and support proceedings.

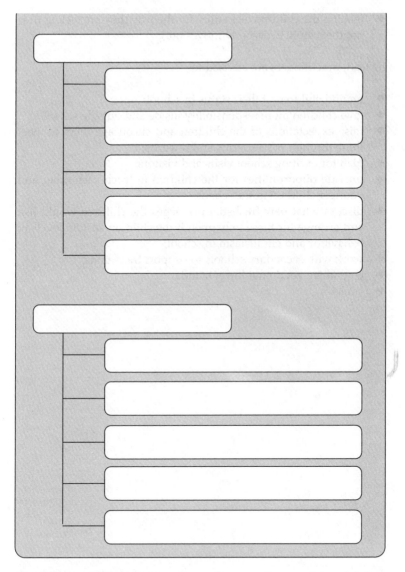

There are a number of strategies and approaches used in school to manage these behaviours yet a number of these are ineffective and should be avoided wherever possible:

◆ punishing the children, e.g. keeping them in at playtime;
◆ taking away their privileges, e.g. being first in the dinner hall;
◆ lecturing the children to 'buck their ideas/attitudes up';

◆ making the children feel guilty for the way they are feeling (it is not their fault; everybody moves on!).

Instead, practitioners are advised to:

◆ remind children of their status in school;
◆ give children more responsibility inside and outside school;
◆ raise expectations of the children and encourage them to meet these through praise, treats and rewards;
◆ plan for exciting school visits and visitors;
◆ provide opportunities for the children to teach each other and younger children in the school;
◆ discuss what new (realistic) privileges the children would like and arrange for these to happen if the children sustain levels of behaviour and enthusiasm in school;
◆ work with secondary schools to support transitions;
◆ empathize yet do not lower standards;
◆ smile!

Behaviours which affect the quality of teaching in the classroom

9. 'Great! Miss isn't here!' Misbehaving for PPA/supply cover

I do PPA/supply cover for a local school and I dread going into particular classes. The children know I am not their main practitioner and so really test me by misbehaving and not completing their work. I am so ashamed of them and of myself sometimes. What can I do?

Year 5 teacher, retired

When a practitioner is away on a training course or absent through ill health some children take this as an opportunity to 'let their hair down' and make the supply practitioner's life a misery. With the introduction of Planning, Preparation and Assessment (PPA) time many children come into contact with a wealth of different adult faces, including teaching assistants, acting as their lead practitioner for an hour or an afternoon, and so it is becoming increasingly important for all practitioners to be able to step into a classroom and manage the behaviour of children whom they do not know.

Interestingly, PPA/supply cover can be very frustrating for the main class teacher when they are greeted by a class of unruly and badly behaved children upon their return. Many children also suffer as they are keen to learn yet are unable to as PPA cover/supply spend their time dealing with 'troublemakers'.

Questions for reflection

Class teacher: How often are you out of the classroom? Do you have to deal with behavioural issues upon your return?

PPA cover: What kinds of behaviour do you have to manage? Do you inform the class teacher about any issues you have had to deal with?

Supply cover: How do you try to manage children's behaviour in a class you have not worked in before? Do you make the class teacher/other staff members aware of any behavioural difficulties you have had during the day?

It is important for us to consider why children see PPA/supply cover as a chance to behave badly:

◆ Inconsistency – PPA/supply cover may not know the rules and routines of the class/setting and so may be more lenient with behaviour.

◆ Lack of respect – most full-time practitioners have earned the respect of the children they teach over a lengthy period of time. PPA/supply cover cannot expect to develop this over an hour/afternoon.

◆ 'Testing the water' – every practitioner knows that a new class will 'test the boundaries' to find out how far they can misbehave until the practitioner reacts. Children working with PPA/supply cover will do this almost immediately.

Issues with PPA/supply cover will occur throughout all of the different key stages although practitioners may experience more behavioural issues in Key Stage 2 as the children are more aware of adults not being '*their* teacher'. So how can we manage this troublesome behaviour?

Activity
Read and mark each of the strategies below using the following key:

✔ You intend to use this.

? You think this is a good idea yet it needs to be adapted slightly for your class.

X You already use this/you have tried this and it does not work.

- ☐ Whenever possible talk to the children the day before you are going to be away. State your expectations about their behaviour while you are away/ask the children to tell you what you expect of them.

- ☐ Ask the PPA/supply cover to write a note stating how well-behaved the children have been for them. Follow this up with rewards and sanctions as and where appropriate the following day.

- ☐ Ask children to self-assess their behaviour upon your return.

- ☐ Use circle time opportunities to discuss the importance of behaving for other adults.

- ☐ Encourage PPA/supply cover to come and work with you for an hour/morning as part of a teaching team so they can see how you manage the behaviour of the children.

- ☐ Highlight key parts of the school's behaviour policy so that PPA/supply cover is aware of school systems for effective behaviour management.

- ☐ During your PPA time casually pop your head into the class to see how well the children are behaving. Ensure the PPA/supply cover knows you are not checking up on them (although you might be!).

- ☐ Ensure PPA/supply cover have all of the correct planning and resources for them to conduct their teaching effectively. Plan stimulating activities for them to undertake – behavioural issues are unlikely to occur if the children have interesting activities to engage with.

- ☐ Consider ways in which children in your class can learn about the 'intrinsic' rewards of behaving well (doing it because they should) and not just the 'extrinsic' (stickers, extra play).

10. 'When you are *quite* ready!' Settling children on the carpet

I dread the beginning of my lessons! It is not because I haven't planned them thoroughly before hand, it's more due to the fact that it takes my class simply ages to settle on the carpet. What can I do about this as it is wasting teaching time and I am getting very frustrated by it!

Year 3 teacher, NQT

Provided there is enough space for a carpet area, most practitioners use carpet areas to bring children together in order to do whole class teaching. Children become familiar with sitting on the carpet when they are in Early Years Foundation Stage, yet it is interesting that children seem to forget the 'Rules of the Carpet' when they either move classes, come back to school after half-term or return to class after playtime!

The Rules of the Carpet

Consider what you think the Rules of the Carpet should be/are. Reflect on your experiences in different classes/schools and what you do with your children at the moment. Make a list of these rules below:

1. _____
2. _____
3. _____
4. _____
5. _____
6. _____

For rules to have any impact on the children's behaviour the following should become an integral feature of their production and usage in the classroom. The rules should be:

- limited in quantity (do you need to cut those above down?);
- limited in the number of words used to express them;
- worded in a positive way, directing the children to what they

should be doing as opposed to identifying the behaviours you do not want to see;
- produced with pictures to give meaning to the words;
- agreed by the adults and children who work in the classroom;
- displayed close to the carpet area so the children can see them clearly;
- referred to every time the children come to the carpet.

Every practitioner will be able to identify behaviours which indicate the children are not settled on the carpet. These include:

- high noise levels;
- finishing off food they did not eat during break time;
- messing about in personal drawers / the cloakroom;
- singing;
- rolling around;
- children chatting to their friends;
- play fighting;
- hanging around the toilets unnecessarily;
- lying on the carpet.

Why is it then that practitioners have to spend time settling the children down before they can begin teaching?

Reason or no reason?
Read the list of reasons presented below and put a tick in the box if you think it influences the children's unsettled behaviour on the carpet or put a cross if you disagree with it.

☐ Temperature
☐ 'Testing' the practitioner
☐ Low practitioner expectations of the children's behaviour
☐ Seeking attention
☐ Children think it is still 'playtime'
☐ Children are trying to resolve issues which happened on the playground
☐ Weather
☐ Additives and preservatives in foods and drinks consumed during playtime

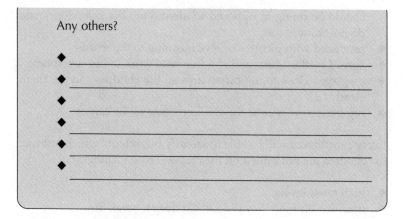

Irrespective of the age of children, this behaviour has the potential to reduce valuable learning and teaching time, disturb other classes and those children wanting to learn in class, and create great anxiety for the practitioner who is desperate to just 'get on with their job'! In educational circles it is said that a great lesson starts with settled and attentive children. So how do you achieve this? Strategies include:

◆ shake a tambourine to grab their attention;
◆ challenge the children to be settled by the time you sit in your chair;
◆ have something interesting for the children to look at as they sit down;
◆ praise those who are settled – can they see anyone as settled as they are?
◆ award stickers and other rewards to the fastest/quietest child to be settled;
◆ ask other practitioners or a parent helper to sit in your chair and monitor the children's behaviour as they come and settle down;
◆ state your expectations when you collect the children from the playground;
◆ have a sand timer in your hand – can the children be all settled and quiet before the sand runs out?
◆ model behaviours you expect to see – sit with your finger on your lips and your back straight, looking at the children;
◆ take one or two minutes off the children's playtime if they continue to come in unsettled – they will soon learn!
◆ clap a rhythm or perform a hand jive to calm the children quickly;
◆ sing a well-known song and ask the children to join in to focus their attention.

11. Wriggle, wriggle, fidget and wriggle!
Restlessness on the carpet

We have one little lad who just cannot settle on the carpet and is forever wriggling about, moving around the outside of the carpet area, fiddling with things in his pocket and other children, and even ending up under the chairs and tables. I wonder if he will ever sit still!

Reception practitioner

Levels of agreement/disagreement

How important do you think it is for children to sit still and listen while you are teaching? Read each of the statements below, recording your level of agreement with the statement in the brackets [ ] using the numerical grading system below:

1 = Strongly agree   4 = Mildly disagree
2 = Agree   5 = Disagree
3 = Mildly agree   6 = Strongly disagree

Children should:

◆ keep their hands and feet to themselves when sat on the carpet [   ]
◆ only be on the carpet for ten minutes at a time [   ]
◆ sit still throughout their time on the carpet [   ]
◆ have a specific sitting space on the carpet and only sit in it [   ]
◆ be made to stand if they are unable to sit still [   ]
◆ sit up straight when sat on the carpet [   ]
◆ be allowed to move from their spot on the carpet if they want to [   ]
◆ not be allowed to sit next to their friends [   ]

While there are no right or wrong responses to the statements above, what the activity is designed to do is to encourage you to critically reflect on your expectations and what you will/will not accept in terms of behaviour on the carpet. Children will not know what your expectations are unless you tell them, either through verbal and/or written strategies. But be warned: while most practitioners have high expectations (which is by no means a bad thing) if they are *too* high, then it will be difficult for children to meet them all of the time. Every class however, irrespective of age, has one or two children who find it difficult to settle down on the carpet. Reasons for this include:

◆ boredom – lack of motivation and interest as the teaching is not pitched at the right level or is not interactive;
◆ medical conditions – ADHD;
◆ reactions to changes – temperature, smells, noise levels, the weather;
◆ sitting close to friends – temptation to talk is increased considerably.

It is easy to spot 'restless' children on the carpet and usually this 'wriggling' is a clear sign that they want to get up and move and do. The best thing to do is move the children onto activities as soon as you can. Trying to teach when children are restless is worthless – both you and the children will become increasingly frustrated with each other.

But how else can you manage this behaviour? Strategies include:

◆ making sure the carpet area is clearly designated. Use masking tape to mark the boundaries;
◆ sitting restless children near to other practitioners or place them right in front of you, near your feet;
◆ regularly reminding the children of the 'Rules of the Carpet';
◆ giving children things to do on the carpet – talking/writing activities;
◆ ensuring all children have been to the toilet before you begin teaching;
◆ asking children to put anything in their pockets in their bag/personal drawer so they are not tempted to fiddle;
◆ establishing 'carpet buddies' who monitor each other's behaviour;
◆ keeping teaching time on the carpet to a minimum – avoid 40-minute epics!

Case Study

One morning a Year 2 teacher introduced her rather restless class to Funky Monkey, a monkey-shaped cushion which the teacher had bought the previous weekend. Funky Monkey 'spoke' to the teacher saying that if any of the children wanted to sit on him then they had to be the 'best sitter' in the class. The teacher asked the children to identify ways in which the children could be deemed 'best sitter' and these were noted on the whiteboard. At the beginning of every day, Funky Monkey was given to the best sitter for the previous day's sitting – all the children wanted to sit on Funky Monkey (which made selecting the best sitter really difficult at times)!

If you like the idea of Funky Monkey yet you are unable to find a monkey-shaped cushion then please do not worry! The idea can be easily adapted as shown in the list below:

◆ purchase a 'colourful cube' from IKEA for the good sitters to sit on;
◆ use carpet squares from samples used by carpet salesmen;
◆ allow good sitters to sit in a hoop (from the PE store);
◆ have a 'special chair' which only the special sitter of the day can sit on.

12. 'Miss! Here! *I* know! Ask *me*! Ask *me*! It's – !' Children who shout out the answers

I use questions to assess the children's learning throughout all of my lessons. I do find it, however, very irritating when children shout out the answer, particularly during whole class teaching. How can I encourage them to keep their answers to themselves?

Reception practitioner

'Shouting out' or 'calling out' is a particularly frustrating behaviour for both practitioners and children in the classroom.

How exactly is it 'frustrating'?

Consider the question above, noting down in what ways shouting out is frustrating for both practitioners and children. Use the table below to record your ideas.

Practitioners	Children

Ask some of your colleagues to share their thoughts and feelings on this topic – do their ideas replicate, challenge or extend your thinking? Ask the children you teach to share their thoughts about shouting out in the classroom. Compare your notes with their ideas.

It is very common for children in the early years to shout out due to the fact they are very keen to please and share their knowledge with others. However, they have not yet mastered the art of putting up their hand to indicate they know the answer – interestingly many children develop this skill yet are still unable to keep the answer to themselves! Shouting out is also likely to occur in Key Stage 1 and lower Key Stage 2 classes, yet while it is less frequent in Years 5 and 6 there are still the occasional incidences!

Managing this behaviour effectively must begin with an investigation into why children shout out.

Challenge the author!

Using your experiences in the classroom see if you can identify more reasons than the author can as to why children shout out answers. Please do not cheat though and look ahead (!). Use the space below to record your ideas.

_____

_____

_____

_____

_____

_____

Once 'starved' of ideas compare your list with mine – how did you do?

Possible reasons include:

◆ excitement – 'I know the answer!';
◆ it just 'slipped out' by accident;
◆ forgetfulness – child forgot routines and manners;
◆ child has not been taught to answer questions correctly – poor role models (practitioners and parents/carers);
◆ seeking attention;
◆ pace of teaching – practitioner has asked a number of questions in quick succession and so the child feels they should answer quickly;
◆ testing the boundaries – child is trying to establish what behaviours the practitioner will/will not tolerate;
◆ medical condition;
◆ peer influences – challenged by friends to irritate the practitioner!

No practitioner likes having children shout out answers while they are in 'mid-flow' as it is extremely rude, can 'put practitioners off' (i.e. make them forget what they were saying), and be frustrating for the children in the class who knew the answer yet were not given the opportunity to share it in the right way because a child blurted it out! Managing this behaviour works on two different levels: *as* it happens and *before* it happens.

As it happens:

◆ use your 'practitioner glare' to indicate your disappointment;
◆ raise your eyebrow at the child – 'Is that how we *usually* answer questions?';
◆ cover your ears with your hands – 'I do not like it when you shout answers at me';
◆ praise children who do put their hand up and patiently wait to give you an answer;
◆ ask a child to remind the rest of the class how you like children to answer questions;
◆ acknowledge the child saying, 'Yes, that is the right answer! I would, however, have liked you to have put you hand up though';
◆ ignore the child and ask another child who *has* put their hand up for their answer.

Before it happens:

- ask the children to think about how you would like them to answer any questions you ask;
- practise answering questions through game play;
- model putting up *your* hand once you have asked a question;
- remind children of your expectations before they put their hands up;
- use thinking time to prevent hands shooting into the air straight-away.

Top Tip!

I taught the children in my Reception class to put one hand up in the air and the other hand over their mouth. This effectively prevented answers being shouted out and meant that any children who were fiddling about with shoelaces and other items would stop doing it!

---

13. *'Swwswsswsswswswwww!'* Children who talk over practitioners

During my main teaching I always seem to catch a couple of children who are talking when I am talking. I use the usual strategies of stopping until they have finished and the 'practitioner glare', yet two seconds later they are at it again! Help me to help them before I lose my rag with them!

Year 4 Teacher covering PPA time

Children who talk when the practitioner is talking is, for many, a real irritation and many of those children who model this behaviour are sure to find themselves in trouble as a result of it due to the fact that:

1   it is extremely rude and discourteous to talk over other people;
2   it breaks up the flow of learning and teaching;
3   it has the potential to disrupt others, waste valuable learning and teaching time, and hinder progress as pupils struggle to engage with work set as they have been unable to hear the practitioner (or they did not listen to them in the first place!).

Questions for reflection
- When during the day do you find children not listening to you?
- Are there any subjects during which the children talk over you?
- Are there particular children in your class who talk over you or is it a whole class issue?
- Do you mind children talking over you during your teaching? If so, why? If not, why not?
- What strategies do you use to manage this behaviour?
- How effective are they in stopping the children talking over you?

We need to be clear about potential reasons as to why children at times talk over practitioners:

- Boredom – poor subject content, delivery or dull practitioner.
- Child is actually checking understanding of the lesson with a peer/friend.
- Rudeness – child is discourteous and has forgotten how to behave.
- Sitting next to their best friend – sometimes a really bad combination.
- Issues from playtime/dinnertime have not yet been resolved for the child.
- Child sees a practitioner talking to a parent helper and believes this is 'the norm'.
- Practitioner is unaware of children talking – lack of observation skills.
- Child is verbalizing their thinking and learning with others.
- Practitioner does not mind children talking over him/her.

As you may have noticed, some of the potential reasons are actually positive and purposeful actions – if the practitioner misinterprets the situation they may be actually doing more harm than good. This is clearly demonstrated in the case study opposite:

Case Study

A Year 2 teacher was working with his class on some word level work relating to the 'oo' phoneme. As the teacher wrote some 'oo' words on the interactive whiteboard he noticed two girls talking to each other.

'I'm glad that you find each other more interesting than my lesson!' he shouted. The teacher demanded the girls stand up and move to different parts of the carpet so they could not talk to each other. The girls sat, ashamed and embarrassed, and did not engage with the rest of the session.

Reflection

What the teacher did not know was that one of the girls was unsure if 'balloon' had the 'oo' phoneme in it. She was a girl of low ability who was asking a more able child to check for her before she put her hand up to offer her idea.

IMPORTANT! Where appropriate, give children the opportunity to explain *why* they were talking to each other as it may just have a direct and positive link to the lesson you are teaching!

Practitioners can manage this troublesome behaviour in a number of ways:

◆ Strategically ignore those talking over you – sometimes they will stop of their own accord.
◆ Encourage children to use peer pressure to stop others talking.
◆ Establish your rule about talking before you start teaching – 'If I am talking then you are listening!'
◆ Ensure friends are not always sitting together.
◆ Use your 'practitioner glare' to silence talkers.
◆ 'Freeze' during your teaching until you see the children stop talking. Unfreeze and continue with the lesson.
◆ Speak to individuals during their group and independent work – do not let them think they got away with it!
◆ Use your voice in different ways to draw the attention of the talkers back to you.
◆ Praise good listeners. Ask them to look out for good listeners for you.

Putting the strategies to the test

Select any two of the strategies above and integrate them into your practice. Review how effective they are after one week.

14. 'Grrrrrrrrr!' Children who interrupt practitioners

If there is one thing that really makes me mad it is children who interrupt me when I am teaching them. There are a couple of children who just cannot seem to help themselves, 'butting in', asking silly questions and generally disrupting the flow and pace of my delivery. What can I do to stop the children from doing this and to also keep myself . . . (breathes deeply) calm?

Year 2 teacher

Of the many behaviours which irritate and upset practitioners there is one which is certain to really get the blood 'boiling', particularly when practitioners are in the middle of some direct teaching – being interrupted. Regarded by many as one of the most rude and obnoxious of behaviours which children 'put into practice', practitioners will naturally find it difficult at times to maintain their professionalism when a child interrupts them.

Questions, questions, questions!

Consider your responses to the following reflective questions:

◆ Who interrupts you in your class?
◆ When do they interrupt you?
◆ Where do they interrupt you?
◆ How exactly do they interrupt you?
◆ Why do they interrupt you?

If you find it difficult to answer any of these questions, ask one of your colleagues to help you reflect on what happens in your class or invite them to come and observe the children when you are teaching.

There are many different ways in which children can interrupt your teaching. These include:

◆ shouting out;
◆ talking over you;
◆ asking an unnecessary question;
◆ telling you something which does not relate to the teaching focus;
◆ giving you a letter/dinner money which should have been handed in at the start of the day;
◆ asking to go to the toilet;
◆ disrupting others by poking those around them, playing with their hair or sitting too closely to their peers;
◆ 'butting in' at inappropriate places during the teaching;
◆ making silly noises or humming.

 Why worry about it?
Consider the implications these behaviours could potentially have on your teaching. Make a list using the bullet points provided below. An example has been given to get you started:

◆ Reduces the natural flow of the taught delivery.
◆ _____
◆ _____
◆ _____
◆ _____
◆ _____

There are many different reasons as to why children interrupt practitioners. In the early years young children act very much on impulse and are keen to verbalize their ideas and thinking at the most inappropriate times. In the primary age phase children may interrupt practitioners because:

◆ they want to – they think it is fun;
◆ they forget their manners (accidentally or deliberately);

◆ they feel threatened by practitioners they work with or the subject being taught;
◆ they are seeking some attention from the practitioner, be it positive or negative;
◆ they have just remembered something and they do not want to forget it;
◆ they feel they have got something valuable to contribute to the lesson yet do not have the skills to share this in the right way;
◆ they are of a nervous habit.

Case Study

A Year 1 teacher found her class had developed the unpleasant habit of interrupting her during her main teaching by making silly 'grunting' noises when they put their hands up to ask/ answer questions. To prevent this she encouraged the children to put their fingers on one hand around their lips so to 'trap' the answer while their other hand was put directly in the air. The teacher said that their extended arms acted as 'aerials' which transmitted the names of those who knew the answer to the invisible antenna located on top of the teacher's brain. This quickly made question and answer sessions very quiet indeed!

There are various strategies to effectively manage this behaviour:

◆ strategically ignore interruptions;
◆ tell the children when they can ask you questions;
◆ provide opportunities for children to talk so they do not do this during your main teaching (unless you want them to!);
◆ deal with any issues before you start teaching;
◆ tell the children to go to the toilet before they come to the carpet;
◆ remind children to use their manners;
◆ hold your hand out as a signal to stop children from interrupting you;
◆ use your 'practitioner glare';
◆ interrupt the children when they speak – do they like it?

Keeping calm

How can you keep yourself calm when dealing with children who interrupt you? Search the internet for three websites which give you at least five strategies to keep those stress levels down!

15. 'Hum hum hum hum hum!' Children who hum in class

I've got a 'hummer' in my class! I can be in the middle of some whole class teaching when I suddenly hear the opening bars of the Harry Potter *theme tune! While it was amusing to start of with it is becoming really distracting and I am fed up of having to stop the flow of my teaching to manage this behaviour – what would you suggest I do?*

Year 4 teacher

Humming is as common a behaviour as eating or drinking – we *all* do it, whether we are listening to music on the radio, watching a TV programme as the signature tune plays, or while we work. Children come into contact with a number of adults in their formative years and see these people humming to themselves – while children recognize that it is an acceptable behaviour what most of them are not aware of is when it is appropriate to hum.

Think about it!

◆ When do children hum in your class?
◆ Why do they do this?
◆ How do children react when you try to stop them?

While many practitioners would not class humming as a serious behaviour issue, it does have the potential to distract adults as they teach and can disturb other children who are trying to listen or concentrate on their work. Knowing why a child might hum to themselves is the first step to effectively managing this behaviour. Possible reasons include:

- the child is bored;
- the child has a 'catchy' tune stuck in her head;
- the child is very musical – 'he shall have music wherever he goes';
- the child is using the tune to help them remember something – *ABC* by the Jackson Five;
- force of habit – the child does it at home;
- the child is expressing his feelings of being happy and contented;
- the child is trying to 'block out' noises e.g. other children talking, 'droning' voice of the practitioner.

But just knowing the reason is unfortunately not enough – we need strategies to prevent the humming becoming an issue for you and the other children in your class.

Scenario

Jake (five years old) is humming the latest number one pop song in the charts to himself as he engages with the maths problems you have set him.

However, he is distracting the rest of the children on his table who cannot concentrate. What would you do?

Consider the range of strategies presented below and highlight any three you would use:

- Use your 'practitioner glare'.
- Place your hand lightly on Jake's shoulder as a gentle reminder.
- Shout at Jake to stop immediately.
- Ask one of the children on the table to tell Jake to kindly stop humming.
- Distract Jake with a sound or an action, e.g. click fingers, shake tambourine.
- Move Jake to a table of his own.
- Gave Jake a verbal warning.
- 'Shhhhhh' Jake!
- Make Jake stand outside for the rest of the lesson.
- Quietly have 'a word' with Jake.
- Remind all of the children in the class of the need for

> quiet working.
> ◆ Strategically ignore it.
> ◆ Explain to Jake why it is not appropriate to hum at this moment in time.
> ◆ Tell Jake of a time later on in the day when he can hum – music lesson, playtime.
> ◆ Take a look at Jake's work, asking him some questions about what he is doing to politely prevent him from

Clearly some of the strategies are ones which practitioners should *avoid* – shouting at the child, for example, is not good practice mainly because the behaviour does not merit this kind of response from you. Children need to be taught when humming to oneself is acceptable and when it is better to keep quiet.

When is it acceptable/unacceptable?

Consider six different times/activities during the school day when children should be made aware of it being acceptable and unacceptable to having a hum to oneself. Use the chart below to record your ideas.

Acceptable	Unacceptable

How would you make children aware of these occasions?

_____

_____

_____

While there is no cure for humming (why would there need to be one?), practitioners should be aware of preventative strategies they can use to save some of their children sounding like frustrated bumble bees!

♦ If you play music in the classroom either play it quietly or choose music the children do not know – pop songs are designed to have catchy rhythms/melodies.
♦ Set expectations for quiet working – asking for silence is virtually impossible and is not healthy for children.
♦ Avoid ignoring it!

16. 'I've . . . forgotten!' Forgetting the answer to questions asked

Why is it when I have a good pace to my lesson there is always one child who holds everything up by putting their hand in the air to answer a question and then say, 'I've forgotten!'? It's really frustrating! How can I manage this behaviour without becoming angry with them?

Trainee teacher working in a Year 2 class

Most children like being actively involved in the learning and teaching which takes place in taught sessions and many achieve this by putting their hand up to answer questions. Some children, however, can be 'too keen' and have a tendency to put their hand up _without_ actually knowing the answer. Inevitably this will reduce the flow of taught sessions if it becomes a regular occurrence. It is therefore important for practitioners to set expectations right from the start and ensure the children know their role in different parts of a lesson, e.g. listeners, active participants, questioners, reviewers.

Reflection and Activity Time!

Take a moment to identify a child in the class in which you work whose hand is quicker than their thinking! Take time to observe/monitor this child, noting when this behaviour occurs during the school day and why. Discuss your observations with others.

An important consideration in the effective management of this behaviour lies in the way in which you react to the situation.

Scenario

Imagine you are delivering the oral and mental starter of a numeracy session. It is fast-paced and against the clock – addition questions are being asked rapidly in an attempt to beat the 17 correct answers given in the three-minute game played yesterday.

Practitioner: What is seven and seven more?
Hands shoot up in the air
Practitioner: Jack! Go for it!
Jack opens his mouth to answer
Jack: Erm . . . erm . . . erm . . .

Do you:

a) move quickly onto someone else to answer the question?
b) support Jack by talking him through a strategy to give an answer?
c) glare at Jack and verbally chastise him later on when the children do not beat the target number of questions?
d) ask someone for the answer and ask Jack if he thought this was the answer?

There is no right or wrong answer to the above scenario as the points below highlight:
Think about it! If you chose:

a) Think about how Jack would feel. He made the effort to put his hand up and you did not really give him a chance to answer.
b) The class would lose out because the time supporting Jack could have potentially answered ten questions.
c) Are you more interested in beating the target or encouraging children to realize it is only a game?
d) Could the rest of the class feel that Jack is gaining credit for someone else's answer, particularly if the other child got it right?

If a number of children seem to regularly forget answers to questions it is important to initially reflect critically on your practice:

◆ Do you give children enough time to answer questions?
◆ Are the questions too difficult for the children to answer?
◆ Do you ask too many questions?
◆ Do you target questions for specific children to answer so they feel involved?
◆ Could you offer better support/advice to 'guide' children to the correct answer?

A number of simple yet effective strategies are on offer to manage this behaviour (see opposite):

Use thinking time – 'I'm going to ask a question and only after I have counted down from three are you able to put your hand up to answer, okay?'	At the start of the lesson encourage children to put their hand up if they know the answer. Use other strategies than hands up – finger on nose, wiggle ears, etc.	Use talking partners so children can share their answers – do they have a shared response?
Encourage children to give you any answer. Turn this into a positive – 'If I had asked what seven and six were then yes, thirteen would have been right!'	Offer children a choice of two answers, one of them being correct – can they select the right one?	Use adult support to help children answer questions. Plan for parts of the lesson when questions will be directed specifically to them so they are ready with the answers.
Differentiate your questions so there are questions for all to answer.	Use a range of open (various responses) and closed (specific answer) questions in your teaching.	Revisit questions in the plenary – does the child now know the answer?

Behaviours which affect the quality of learning in the classroom

17. 'Eh? What? Where? Why? What's that?' Children and concentration in the classroom

Whether I am doing whole class teaching, small group work or one-to-one with a particular child, he seems unable to remain focused on the task in hand, constantly being distracted by sounds and movements made by the other children in the class. What can I do to build up his concentration levels?

Year 2 teacher

Most of the learning children acquire in school requires them to stay focused and concentrate on what is being told to them/what they are doing. As children progress through the key stages it is important for them to have built up good levels of concentration for them to cope with the complex demands of the subject areas they will study. There are, however, children whose attention span remains quite limited and who struggle to remain focused, particularly if the environment provides lots of distractions!

Con . . . cen . . . trate!

◆ How many children are there in your class who you would say have a limited attention span?
◆ How easily do distractions affect their ability to concentrate?
◆ What specific distractions interfere with their concentration levels? Make a note of these.
◆ What effect does this limited attention span have on the children's academic achievements?
◆ Are there specific subject areas they are underperforming/excelling in? Why do you think this is the case?

Every class will have one or more children who suffer from a limited attention span and it more likely to be males who demonstrate this behaviour due to biological factors, i.e. levels of testosterone. This is not to say that some girls will not have low concentration levels as *any* form of distraction can disturb even the most focused children. These distractions include:

♦ children being taken out of class for music lessons, Early Literacy Support;
♦ messages being brought to practitioners by children from other classes;
♦ parent helpers and visitors walking in and out of classrooms;
♦ children coming into class late;
♦ colourful and moving displays;
♦ sounds and movement outside the classroom, e.g. birds singing, cars driving past the school, workmen digging up the road;
♦ practitioners and students completing jobs around the classroom as the children engage in whole class learning.

Limiting the effects of distractions

Consider ways in which you could prevent the distractions listed above from disturbing the children in your class. Record your ideas and share them with colleagues. Put some of them into practice and evaluate their effectiveness – set a review date by when you will critically reflect on their impact: _____

We must remember, however, that concentration levels are not solely affected by distractions. Other factors include:

♦ maturation;
♦ temperature and weather conditions;
♦ general state of health and well-being;
♦ amount of sleep/exercise the child has had;
♦ types/amount of food and drink the child has consumed;
♦ issues at home which may be playing on the child's mind;
♦ time of day;
♦ type of activity the child is engaging in;
♦ diet.

These, in essence, are the warning signs for practitioners to be aware of as they will find that the concentration levels of a young child will be low if it is Friday afternoon, they are not feeling well and it is cold and wet outside!

To maintain and build concentration levels practitioners are encouraged to dip into this selection of strategies:

◆ Plan for exciting activities, both whole class and table top.
◆ Use ICT applications to sustain concentration levels.
◆ Integrate children's interests into your teaching and their learning.
◆ Teach in short bursts to avoid concentration levels dwindling.
◆ Use brain breaks to keep the children attentive.
◆ Team teach with other practitioners, students and parent helpers to keep the children 'hooked'.
◆ Observe children with low concentration levels during free play – what activities do they like doing which hold their attention? Plan for the use of these.
◆ Praise and reward children who sustain and improve their concentration levels.
◆ Ensure measures are taken to avoid distracting the children during teaching time.

Top Tip!
One strategy I developed with a colleague was for a little boy who was unable to concentrate on anything at all. By pointing to our eyes with two fingers on one hand we would say, 'Philip – focus!' This quickly attracted his attention and kept him attentive until the next distraction came along!

18. 'Erm . . . er . . . umm . . . what?'
Forgetfulness in the classroom

There are two children (a boy and a girl) in my class who are just so forgetful! They forget where they last left their pencils, cannot remember instructions given out two seconds previously and both seem to have no idea of where their seat is in class (you know, the ones they have been sitting in all year!). What can I do to help them 'remember'?

Year 1 teacher

Reflection time

◆ How often do you forget things?

◆ What sort of things do you forget – big things (where your house is, the name of your partner) or little things (telephone numbers, where you last put your keys)?

◆ How do you try to overcome this forgetfulness? Make a note of strategies you use to help you:

_____

_____

_____

_____

_____

_____

Is it possible to remember and recall everything? As the activity above clearly shows we all have forgotten things at one time or another even though most of us have pretty good memories. With this in mind, if a child appears to be forgetful on a regular basis, then there is probably a good reason for it. These include:

Child has a general lack of organizational skills.	Child is reluctant to take responsibility for her own actions.	Child has overcontrolling parents – the child does not have to remember.
Child has learning difficulties.	Child is absentminded by nature.	Child has other things on his mind.

Take a moment to think! Is it that they really cannot remember or that they do not try to remember?

If you have children who are very forgetful and this is having an effect on their ability to retain learning acquired in school it is important that these children are placed on the Special Educational Needs (SEN) register whereby they have an Individual Education Plan (IEP) which will establish clear targets, action to take and dates for review. Severe learning needs may result in them being statemented.

Activity

Talk to your SEN co-ordinator (SENCO) about the processes involved in formulating IEPs and statements. Consider children you work with who would benefit from some specific action and support by using these processes.

Remember! If a child is forgetful and seems confused, drowsy, unable to focus or is momentarily 'not there', then medical support should be sought immediately. These may be signs of a physical condition (hearing loss, epilepsy) or a psychological matter.

All children will demonstrate signs of forgetfulness and this may be due to simple things including:

◆ tiredness;
◆ hunger;
◆ boredom;
◆ restlessness;
◆ too many instructions given by the practitioner;
◆ distracted by others.

Think box!

Here are some good questions to ask yourself if children become forgetful in your class:

◆ What time of day is it? Most children begin to switch off near the end of the afternoon.

◆ How hot/cold is it in the classroom? Temperature has an effect on children being able to remember things.

◆ Am I putting unnecessary stresses and strains on the children? Too much work, too many instructions or too much information can cause children to forget.

◆ Is the work set suitable to the children's needs and abilities? Complicated worksheets or tasks with many parts can confuse children.

◆ Have I made it clear as to what I want the children to do? Instructions delivered quickly or in a random order make it very difficult for children to remember them!

To manage forgetfulness in the classroom practitioners can use any the following strategies:

◆ Structure the day – tell the children what will be happening, use picture/words cards to help them to visually remember.

◆ Make sure items (e.g. pencils) are always set out and returned to where they belong in the classroom.

◆ Play forgetful! Ask children to retell you things you have just instructed them to do to assess if they have been listening.

◆ Praise children for remembering to do something.

◆ Model strategies (refer to Reflection time task on page 56) to help *you* remember things – write notes on yellow labels, scribble messages on the corner of the board, draw pictures of objects on paper.

◆ Create a 'Remember Board' on which can be pinned words, labels, pictures or objects to help the class remember things, e.g. the special assembly at 10 am TODAY!

◆ Tell stories about imaginary characters that are forgetful. Talk about the importance of being 'on the ball'.

◆ Ask children to remind you to take the register, sing a song, and give out letters at the end of the day. Did *they* remember?

Message boards are a great way to inform children about things that are happening in the setting (and to remind practitioners as to what is going on too!). Use them regularly to ensure their effective use.

19. 'I *can't!*' The child who thinks she cannot do anything

Why is there always one child who constantly says that they 'can't' do something? No matter what work I give a particular girl to do, all she ever says is 'I can't do that!' Apparently she can't paint, do maths sums or write letters! It's driving me potty!

Year 6 teacher

In most classes there will be a child who has developed the 'I can't' syndrome – an automatic reaction when they are faced with a new challenge or activity to undertake. Directly linked to the child's self-esteem, confidence and ability levels, this behaviour has the potential to really hold children back and prove challenging for practitioners who have to offer excessive amounts of support, encouragement and advice to coax these children into thinking that they can do it.

Activity

Why do you think children say 'I can't'? Record your ideas in the grid below:

Compare your thoughts to those provided at the end of this section.

One potential reason relates to children who are simply lazy – saying 'I can't' is a way for idle children to get out of having to do work. Most practitioners are usually concerned about children who say 'I can't' and so may offer support and time in helping them to complete their work. Do take care that lazy children do not take your time up unnecessarily.

Strategies to manage this behaviour include:

◆ setting the children clear targets relating to how much work you want to see from them and when;
◆ frequently monitoring their progress;
◆ praising them for working well;

◆ setting and sharing high expectations – make sure the children know when they have achieved them;
◆ ensuring children who unnecessarily do not complete their work on time are given an appropriate sanction – they will soon learn!;
◆ giving children an egg timer – 'Time Targets!'

For most children, saying 'I can't' is a clear sign they are frightened. It could be a fear of, for example:

◆ the subject/area being studied;
◆ the task/activity being set;
◆ the time being given to complete work;
◆ the expectations of the practitioner;
◆ feeling they will fail.

This fear can be noted in children in a number of ways:

◆ the child's body tenses up – shoulders are raised, arms are wrapped around body for comfort;
◆ the child uses avoidance/diversionary tactics to get out of work;
◆ the child stutters or mumbles;
◆ the child becomes emotionally upset – tears, lip quivering;
◆ the child's facial expressions show apprehension and fear.

Children of all ages are prone to developing this behaviour if they do not feel safe, well-supported and able in their learning environment. Ways in which practitioners can ensure children feel that they *can* do and achieve in their classroom include:

◆ Develop an 'I can!' approach to learning and teaching – have a little chant to empower children, e.g. 'Can we do it?' 'YES, WE CAN!'
◆ Empathize with children – appreciate their apprehensions and concerns regarding the work set.
◆ Praise something a child can do.
◆ Make children 'experts of the class', playing to their strengths, e.g. use good football players to demonstrate ball skills to the rest of the children.
◆ Record children's 'can' achievements regularly.
◆ Offer support but do not do everything for the child – give them space and time to try and do things for themselves.
◆ Talk to parents/carers about activities which elicit the 'I can't' response – do they have a similar issue at home?
◆ Display examples of all the children's work.

Answers to Activity

There are many reasons as to why children say 'I can't'. These include:

◆ low self-esteem/low confidence levels;
◆ fearful of 'getting it wrong' and being made to feel stupid in front of their peers;
◆ fearful of the repercussions if they do make a mistake – being told off, struck;
◆ tiredness or lack of energy;
◆ laziness – child realizes practitioners will 'help' them without having to put in any real effort;
◆ poor understanding of the task – not pitched at the right level for the child's ability and stage of development;
◆ frightened of the task – too much to complete in the time given, work explores a new concept which the child does not fully understand (e.g. long division!);
◆ an automatic reaction – child's mind set or general attitude is very negative;
◆ task could be 'meaningless' to the child – you must provide some sense of meaning and realism to all tasks set by linking them to LIFE.

20. Oh so laaaazzzzzzzzzy! Lazy children in the classroom

While most of my class busy themselves with painting, drawing, writing and game play there is one girl who is just lazy and does absolutely nothing! I sometimes think breathing is a struggle for her! Her work books are virtually empty – I've tried everything but it is (in her words) ' . . . such an effort!' Help me!

Year 1 teacher

Most children are excited about learning and have a thirst for knowledge and understanding. Every class, however, will have one or two children who are just 'bone idle' – those who find the thought of work a painful chore and who simply cannot be bothered. While we all, at one time or the other, have felt this way, it can become an unfortunate way of life for some children and a real issue if their inability to engage adequately with activities begins to hinder their progress.

Reflective questions

◆ How many children in your class would you describe as being 'lazy'?

◆ What factors influence these children to model this lethargic behaviour?

◆ How do you attempt to manage this behaviour?

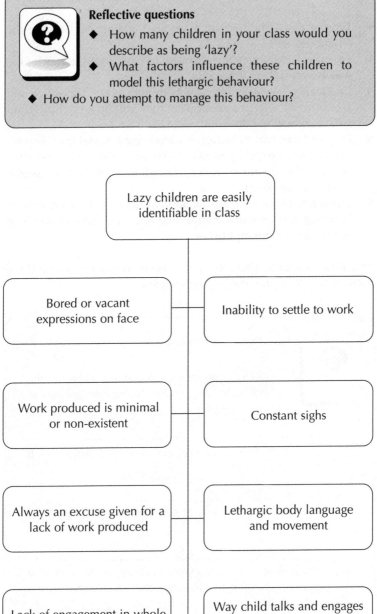

Lazy children are easily identifiable in class

Bored or vacant expressions on face

Inability to settle to work

Work produced is minimal or non-existent

Constant sighs

Always an excuse given for a lack of work produced

Lethargic body language and movement

Lack of engagement in whole class or small group work

Way child talks and engages with others is drawn out and heavy

So why are some children lazy? Possible reasons include:

◆ Time of day – children are more tired and appear 'lazy' in the afternoon.
◆ Poor diet – child may not eat much or have access to much food which makes them lethargic.
◆ Personality – some children are born with a lazy disposition and are naturally selective about what they will do (very little!) and what they will not do (a lot!).
◆ Peer and parental influences – friends may model lazy dispositions which the child perceives to be acceptable, child may have parents who are out of work (although this does not necessarily mean they are lazy).
◆ Environment – areas of social deprivation may drive children to believe that no amount of effort will help them achieve anything so they do not attempt to try.

Practitioners should also reflect on their own practice in the classroom as this may promote lazy tendencies.

Questions to ask yourself

1. Do you promote independent skills in the classroom or are the children dependent on you doing something for them?

2. How much do you support children who struggle with their work?

3. How much time do you give children to complete their work?

4. How high are your expectations relating to the amount of work the children are to produce each lesson and the quality of it?

If you answered
1. Independent
2. A little
3. 20 minutes
4. High
to the questions
above then
please read ➞

We should promote independent skills in all children irrespective of their age.

Striking that balance between supporting children in their work and doing it for them is difficult – use assessment data and observations to help you identify what children can and cannot do.

Having specific yet realistic time limits for engaging with work is important – keep children aware of time limits.

High expectations are essential – if too high then children will not try because they know they will fail so make them realistic and achievable.

If you answered
1. Dependent
2. A lot
3. As much as
they need
4. Dependent on
the child
to the questions
above then
please read ➞

Develop independent skills in your class by establishing job monitors.

If children depend on you to do something and you are not there, then it will not get done! Too much support promotes laziness as children realize that you will help them until the work is finished.

Do set yourself time limits otherwise you will spend the whole lesson with one child. Have clocks around the classroom so children know when they should finish their work by.

Do ensure expectations are consistent for all children so that they feel equal in the class.

Set appropriate work so all children can engage with it.

If your answers
were a mixture of
the previous two
sections then
please read ➞

Every practitioner works in a different way depending on their class and the time of year.

Suitable independence, appropriate support, adequate time limits and consistent expectations will help to keep lazy children 'on their toes'.

Always work *with* children as working *against* them will make them become lazy all the more.

So . . . how can we manage their behaviour?

◆ Give lazy children little tasks to complete, building these up in terms of time and complexity.
◆ Use part of play and dinnertime if necessary to catch up on work complete. Send work home if appropriate.
◆ Praise children for active engagement with work.
◆ Use peer and self-assessment to appraise effort, quantity and/or quality levels in work undertaken.

21. WHOOOOOOOSH! 'Finished!'
The child who rushes his work

A little boy in my class is always rushing his work! He never takes his time with anything he has to produce – everything is so . . . scribbly! He will hand me his work for approval after about 30 seconds of being set the task! How can I encourage him to take care and pride in his work?

Year 1 teacher

There are children who seem to think that doing the bare minimum in the quickest time possible is acceptable. Even when practitioners share high expectations with the children for their work, there are always those who will produce a squiggle on the page and claim it to be a 'detailed drawing of a car', or complete all of the numeracy sums set in five minutes flat even though all of their answers are wrong.

Children of all ages are prone to rushing their work for a number of reasons if they:

◆ have a short attention span and are desperate to move onto other things;
◆ are uninterested or unstimulated by the activity set;
◆ have been brought to an activity from one they were totally engrossed in – the child wants to get back to it as quickly as possible;
◆ are aware of a more exciting task to undertake after they have completed their work – using the computer, playing with the musical instruments;
◆ are desperate to be 'first in the line' for completing their work first;
◆ have to complete their work quickly before the bell sounds for dinner/assembly;
◆ the task is not pitched at the right level for them – too hard/easy.

Reflection time!

Interestingly, the last two points above relate to issues surrounding practitioners' poor planning and time management. Reflect on your own practice in the classroom during a normal day which could influence children to rush their work unnecessarily.

◆ Do you set too much work for the children to undertake in the time available?

◆ Is the work pitched at the right level for the children? How do you know?

◆ Do you give enough time warnings during the lesson to indicate how much time is left to complete their work?

While it might not be your practice which is at fault, it is inevitable that you will have experience of children who continuously come back to show you their work even though you keep sending them back to:

a) improve their pictures;
b) check their spellings;
c) add more to their work;
d) show their workings out;
e) check their use of capital letters and full stops.

Often it only took them three minutes to produce it in the first place! This can become tiresome for both you and the child. So how can you prevent this from happening?

Give children time to think/plan their work before they start.	Ensure children do not put pen to paper until they are clear about what they have to do.	Only allow children to draw pictures when you are happy with their written work.
Set high expectations for their work before you set them to the task.	Share success criteria relating to the learning objectives, so the children are aware of what you are expecting from them.	Use peer assessment strategies before the children show you their work – do their peers think the work is good enough?

Children who rush their work are usually asked by practitioners to go back and add more/improve it. Most children will either make more of a mess of it or become upset and refuse to do any more to it. Strategies need to be readily available to manage this situation appropriately. But which ones are appropriate/inappropriate? You decide!

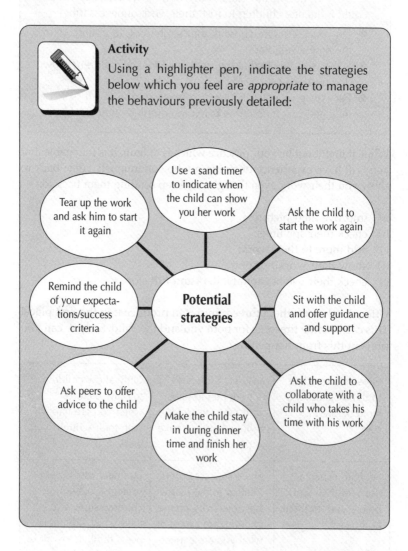

Activity

Using a highlighter pen, indicate the strategies below which you feel are *appropriate* to manage the behaviours previously detailed:

Tear up the work and ask him to start it again

Use a sand timer to indicate when the child can show you her work

Ask the child to start the work again

Remind the child of your expectations/success criteria

Potential strategies

Sit with the child and offer guidance and support

Ask peers to offer advice to the child

Make the child stay in during dinner time and finish her work

Ask the child to collaborate with a child who takes his time with his work

If you want children to take their time with their work there are a number of strategies you can use to ensure this happens:

◆ Ensure you provide the children with enough time to complete the task set.
◆ Only tell children what extension tasks they can undertake once you are satisfied with the work produced.
◆ Make verbal comments about children who are working steadily, showing their work so that 'rushing' children slow down.
◆ Model careful and steady working behaviours in your teaching.
◆ Help 'rushing' children to set short targets, breaking the work up into small yet manageable sections.
◆ Display carefully produced work.
◆ Set the children off on one part of the task and then add more information at short intervals.

22. Plod Plod! Tick Tock! Plod Plod!
The child who takes *for ever* to complete his work

I always make sure the children in my class are given sufficient time to complete their work. However, there is one child who simply takes for ever to finish his work – I could give him a day to finish one piece of work and he still would not manage it! What can I do about this?

Year 2 teacher

Every class has one or more children who seem to take an eternity to complete a piece of work. It is not that they are necessarily lazy – it is just that everyone else seems to finish the work within the time set, while these children have barely written a sentence or (even worse) the date! This is a frustrating behaviour because these children's workbooks never really show the child's full potential and are usually littered with written comments including 'See me!', 'This is not enough work!' or 'Two sentences in one hour is not good enough!'

Turning the negatives into constructive positives

Written comments in children's books should be a balance of praise and targets for future work. Consider the comments made on the children's work above and rewrite them so they are more constructive in terms of giving the children something to work towards. Use the space below to record your ideas.

_____

_____

_____

_____

_____

_____

_____

_____

Show these to one of your colleagues – how would they have phrased these comments?

Clearly there is more than one reason as to why some children take for ever to complete a piece of work. These include:

- being a perfectionist;
- does not understand the task;
- easily distracted;
- bored by the work set;
- unwell;
- hot or cold (in response to the weather);
- sitting next to friends – chatting with others;
- in need of adult support;
- too much work to be completed in time given;
- tired;
- practitioner's expectations are too high;

◆ lazy;
◆ repetitive task – all paper-based 'death by worksheet' learning;
◆ lack of organization – child does not have all the right equipment to complete the task (child or practitioner's fault);
◆ not enough time given to complete task.

If practitioners are observant enough they will be able to spot the warning signs of children who will take for ever to complete their work.

Find out!

Observe a child for one lesson in your class, ideally an extended writing session. Make a note of all the different ways the child 'fills in time' which prevents them from putting pen to paper. Use the space below to record your observations:

_____

_____

_____

_____

_____

_____

Possible warning signs you may have noted include:

Unnecessary sharpening of pencil.	Looking out of the window.	Spending ages searching for words in the dictionary/ thesaurus.
Talking to peers at table.	Incessant rubbing out of work from off the page.	Frequent visits to the toilet.

There are a number of effective ways in which practitioners can ensure children who take for ever to complete their work manage to complete it on time:

◆ Share clear expectations in both verbal and written form.
◆ Set children who need more time to complete their work to task first.
◆ Ensure adult support is nearby to encourage and motivate children.
◆ Establish time limits – ensure children are given five/two minute warnings.
◆ Set individual targets for the child, e.g. 'I would like to see two sentences by the time I come back in four minutes time . . . '
◆ Offer incentives for children to complete the work without unnecessarily rushing it, e.g. extra playtime, free choice activities.
◆ Use sticker charts to record effort levels which work towards a reward of the child's choice.

Warning! Many practitioners keep children in during playtime and dinnertime to complete work they have not finished in class. While this can be an effective 'deterrent' strategy, those who consistently do not finish their work on time will spend most of their school life inside! This is not healthy and can make the child quite resentful of the practitioner.

Required action! Ensure time is found during other sessions for work to be finished or that it is sent home to be completed.

Think!
Sometimes the practitioner is the reason why a child is unable to complete their work on time. To prevent this happening practitioners should:

◆ keep to time, particularly when teaching;
◆ provide support as and where necessary;
◆ ensure work is differentiated appropriately;
◆ ensure all resources are to hand;
◆ vary work set – verbal, written and practical form.

23. Too the loo!
Children who make frequent visits to the toilet

There is one girl in my class who makes an alarming number of requests to go to the toilet during the school day, particularly during learning and teaching time, and this is having a real effect on the quality and quantity of work she produces in class. I'm not always convinced she needs to 'go' but I don't want to have to mop up any 'puddles'! Can you help me?

Year 2 teacher

Making lots of visits to the toilet is usually an indication of one of two things:

1. The child is suffering from a water infection.
2. The child is using these visits as an avoidance tactic to get out of doing something.

This kind of behaviour is quite common in all three key stages and is applicable to both boys and girls. There are, however, many reasons as to why children do this, and these can be quite age specific.

Sorting the reasons

Sort the different reasons overleaf (using the capital letter reference) into the table below so it is specific to a particular key stage. If you feel it appropriate you can use the reason in two or all of the columns.

EYFS	KS1	KS2

A. Work set is too easy or too hard.
B. Child is fascinated by toilets.
C. Child has a short attention span.
D. Vanity – child likes to look at himself in the mirrors.
E. Child needs more kinaesthetic learning opportunities.
F. Child is ill – water infection, diarrhoea.
G. Child is making herself sick – suffering from bulimia.
H. Child dislikes the subject being studied.
I. Child thinks going to the toilet is a game.
J. Child has a weak bladder.
K. Child has a compulsive disorder linked to cleanliness – needs to be constantly washing hands and face.
L. Child does not understand what he has to do with the work.
M. Restlessness.
N. Child is suffering from period pains.
O. Child likes the privacy provided by the cubicle.
P. Child likes to play with the hand driers or the soap dispenser.
Q. Child wants a private 'chat' with a friend.
R. Child is attention seeking.
S. Child is attracted by something in the toilets – displays, smells, sounds.
T. Child has discovered the pleasure of manipulating their sexual organs.

Making lots of visits to the toilet can cause issues for everyone in the classroom as it can:

a) disrupt the practitioners' flow of teaching;
b) disturb the concentration of other children in class;
c) be detrimental for the child making the visits as he may miss valuable pieces of information/instructions while being out of the classroom.

With this in mind practitioners need a range of strategies to ensure this behaviour does not impact on learning and teaching. From a day-to-day perspective the following are useful:

- Ensure there are regular opportunities for children to go to the toilet during the day – have a routine before and after lessons.
- Keep a mental log of the number of times children go to the toilet.
- Use other practitioners in the classroom to observe who makes frequent visits and when they do this.
- Ensure work set is pitched at the right level.
- Say to the child she can go after she has completed her work.
- Offer adult support for children who need it to keep them 'on task'.

Top Tip!

Many practitioners use the classic 'Just wait five minutes' strategy as they know some children simply 'try it on'. But be warned: the child may be actually telling the truth! Always have spare underwear and clothing if children do have a toilet accident in class. To prevent this happening, however, it is sometimes better to give children the benefit of the doubt.

If you think a child has a water infection:

- Talk to the child – does he think he has a problem?
- Talk to parents and carers about your concerns.
- Speak to your local GP for advice.

There are a number of effective strategies which you can put in place to prevent this behaviour ever becoming an issue:

- Have clear toilet rules which are devised in collaboration with the children. Ensure these are displayed outside and inside the toilet area.
- Remove any 'distractions' – pictures, music, displays and newspapers on the toilet doors.
- Prop the toilet door open slightly so you can monitor noise levels and the number of children using the facilities.
- Have toilet monitors (Year 5/6 children) particularly during break/dinnertimes.

24. 'You're late! You're late! For a very important . . . lesson!' Children who arrive late to class

I am a real stickler for time – when the bell sounds for the start of school my class go straight in. After the register has been taken we get straight to work yet 20 minutes later Clive saunters into class without a care in the world. He always has the same excuse (overslept!) yet his education is really suffering – what can I do about this?

Year 1 teacher

Children who arrive late to school have the potential to be very disruptive to the start of the day as they:

♦ cause issues for school administrators when totalling the number of dinners/sandwiches for the day;
♦ disturb other children's learning as they enter/settle into class;
♦ interfere with the flow of the practitioner's delivery;
♦ force practitioners to unnecessarily repeat information to keep the child 'up to speed' with the rest of the class.

Reflective questions

♦ How many children do you have in your class who frequently turn up to school late?
♦ Why is this? What reasons do the children give for their lateness?
♦ When do you ask children to explain why they are late – as they arrive, once they are settled on the carpet, or as they work?
♦ What measures have you put in place to ensure children arrive at school on time?
♦ How effective are these?

Consider the strategies suggested below to support your practice.

Children of all ages are prone to arrive late to school. Most children manage to get to school on time, so why is it that not everyone can manage it? Reasons include:

◆ disorganized parents and children;
◆ oversleeping;
◆ child care support arrives late or is ill;
◆ child is left to sort himself out – unconscious of the time;
◆ child had an early appointment which overran – dentist, doctors;
◆ family difficulties – divorce, separation, newborn baby;
◆ car breaks down on the way to school;
◆ issues with the traffic – accidents, congestion;
◆ parents have to drop children off at different schools (secondary and primary) at the same time.

There are more reasons which I am sure you would be able to identify.

Practitioner challenge!

Try to beat a colleague at a game of 'Excuses, Excuses, Excuses!' Face each other and take it in turns to identify as many excuses as you can as to why children may arrive late to school. The loser is the one who either repeats an excuse already mentioned or 'dries up' whereas the winner . . . isn't!

While practitioners need to effectively manage children when they arrive to school late, they need to also consider ways to prevent this behaviour becoming a regular occurrence. Strategies include:

Child's late arrival	Prevention
◆ Acknowledge the child – most of the time it is not his fault he is late. ◆ Use other practitioners or parental support to take the child's coat and bags. ◆ Ask the child to join the rest of the class as soon as she can.	◆ Raise your concerns with the headteacher – could she speak to the parents/carers? ◆ Monitor the number of times the child is late on a weekly basis. ◆ Speak to parents/carers – make them aware of how

◆ At appropriate points ask the class to review what they have been learning about so far to check they have been listening and help the 'late' child get 'up to speed'.

◆ Speak to the child once he begins his work at his desk – check if he is okay and see if you can help him in any way.

◆ Smile!

disruptive it is for the school and the child.

◆ Write letters to the parents/ carers expressing your concerns.

◆ Inform Education Welfare Officers.

◆ Ensure newsletters document the importance of children being on time at the start of the day.

◆ Use PSHCE and circle time sessions to discuss the importance of good time-keeping.

It is important to remember that everyone turns up late for something at one time or another – sometimes it is unavoidable. Practitioners will find that children who arrive late to school were probably arriving late last year and will be next year if strategies are not put in place to manage it. A kindly word of support to parents/ carers is usually effective, but they do need to know that social services could be called to deal with the situation leading to a possible prosecution if their children are not brought to school on time.

4

Behaviours on the playground

25. Fisticuffs! Children who fight in the playground

It always seems to happen when I'm on the playground – a fight breaks out and I seem to be the only person on duty! I think I handle the situation quite well but five minutes later those involved seem to be fighting again – clearly I am not doing a good job! What is the best way to deal with an outbreak of fighting on the playground?

Year 1 teacher

Fights can occur anywhere and at any time, although many seem to happen when children are on the playground. Children are automatically drawn to a fight; for some reason a large crowd will encircle those having 'a scrap' and the chanting of 'Fight! Fight!' will usually reach your ears before you see the fight actually taking place – try keeping your eyes open!

Start with the negatives!
What do you think the Year 1 teacher is doing which is ineffective in managing this 'fighting' behaviour? Make a list of possible practices you would avoid using when a fight breaks out on your playground:

_____

_____

_____

_____

Children from the ages of three to 11 will engage in 'fighting' behaviours at one time or another and it is more common for boys to fight each other than girls, although the actual behaviours they exhibit are somewhat different. Fights on the playground will usually involve two or more children and have different levels of severity depending on what the children are actually doing, be it pushing, pulling, prodding, striking, kicking, punching, biting, pulling hair, scratching or a combination of two or more or all of the above.

Why oh why oh why?
Take a look at the possible reasons as to why children fight each other, ticking those you agree with and putting a cross next to those you disagree with.

◆ Frustration [   ]
◆ Fun thing to do [   ]
◆ Way to gain practitioner's attention [   ]
◆ Peer/sibling influence – name calling [   ]
◆ Self-defence [   ]
◆ Children are playing a game which got out of hand [   ]
◆ Media influences – recently watched the film Fight Club [   ]
◆ Reaction to a rise or fall in temperature [   ]
◆ Emotional illness which the child cannot control [   ]
◆ Poor social/communication skills [   ]
◆ Issues at home which the child cannot cope with [   ]
◆ Seen as a way to show others their masculine traits [   ]

When asked, the Year 1 teacher was rather vague about how she attempted to manage fighting incidences on the playground, saying that she:

◆ told the children to stop fighting;
◆ made the children sit away from each other on the benches;
◆ asked the children to explain why they were fighting;
◆ spoke to the children about fighting being an inappropriate thing to do.

It is not clear how long the practitioner kept the children sitting on the benches and when she asked them to explain why they were fighting – straight after the incident? After they had been on the benches for a while? How long did she speak to the children about fighting being an inappropriate thing to do – two minutes? An hour? Was it a quick reminder or a lecture with PowerPoint slides?

Clearly a much tighter, more specific set of strategies need to be in place to manage fighting incidents more effectively. But what are they and in what order should they be done?

I'll provide the strategies, you provide the order!

Order the strategies (1–12) below so you have a comprehensive sequence of strategies to help manage incidences when children are caught fighting on the playground:

☐ Walk towards the fight – do not run.

☐ Keep sentences short and to the point.

☐ Ask a child to go and get help, i.e. other members of staff.

☐ Avoid making physical contact with either child wherever possible.

☐ Listen to both sides of the story before you decide what you are going to do.

☐ Talk in a calm yet firm voice.

☐ Ask onlookers to go and play elsewhere.

☐ Allow children to calm down before you ask them why they were fighting.

☐ Blow a whistle to get the children's attention if needed.

☐ Send the children inside to the headteacher.

☐ Use the children's names if you know them. If not ask children nearby to identify them.

☐ Position yourself between the children if you can.

☐ Return calmly to your duties as quickly as possible.

26. HIY *YAA!* Children who kick others

For most children at my school playtime it is a great opportunity to blow off steam and have some fun. However, there are a few children who have started deliberately kicking other children for no reason at all, yet one of our school rules clearly states that 'We will not hurt each other'. What can I do about this?

Year 3 teacher

Points for reflection

Reading the above description should highlight two key things in the reader's mind:

1. Clearly the school rules are not working; the children either have forgotten them or are deliberately breaking them – why is this?
2. The school as a whole should be working together to manage this behaviour, not just one person.

Kicking others is a particularly unpleasant behaviour as it has the potential to cause serious physical harm, e.g. bruising, bleeding or the breaking of bones. No child likes to be kicked and it is clearly a behaviour which needs to be managed effectively and efficiently so children do not have to endure the pain it causes.

Go on then . . . do my job!

Here is your opportunity to test your ability as a potential contributing author to this book. Without looking at the answers opposite, answer the following questions as fully as you can on a separate piece of paper:

A. Why do children kick others?
B. Do more girls or boys kick others or is there a balance between the sexes?
C. What strategies would you use to manage children who kick others?
D. Who should you attend to first – the child who has kicked another or the child who has been kicked? Why?

Let's see how you did!

Answers to A: Why do children kick others?

◆ Frustration.
◆ Anger – aggression.
◆ Attention seeking.
◆ Learned behaviour from peers or siblings.
◆ Lack of modelled practice of sharing or turn-taking.
◆ Form of self-defence.
◆ Accidental – missed the football.
◆ Poor gross motor skills.
◆ Practice – child is learning how to kick in his after-school kung-fu club.
◆ Copying others they have seen, e.g. film stars including Jackie Chan and Keanu Reeves, and football stars, e.g. David Beckham and Wayne Rooney.
◆ Way to dominate and bully others.
◆ Game – 'Can you dodge my leg swing?'

Answers to B: Do more girls or boys kick others or is there a balance between the sexes?

In the early years practitioners will find that both boys and girls kick others as their limited grasp of language means they will resort more quickly to physical means of showing their anger and frustration. As children progress into Key Stage 1 and 2 practitioners find that boys are more likely to kick others although girls may kick others when engaged in 'cat fights'.

Answers to C: What strategies would you use to manage children who kick others?

◆ Use time out.
◆ Make children apologize to each other.
◆ Talk about the feelings of those they have kicked.
◆ Tell the child that 'only donkeys kick'.
◆ Remind the child of the school rules and expectations.
◆ Allow the child to explain her actions – accidental or on purpose?
◆ Ask the child to consider how he would feel if someone kicked him.
◆ Discourage the child from playing games which involve kicking in any shape or form.

◆ Send the child inside if her kicking continues.
◆ Speak to parents/carers about concerns.
◆ Catch the child being good later on – promote behaviours you want to see.
◆ Use PHSCE and circle time opportunities to examine the dangers and feelings associated with kicking and of being kicked.

Answers to D: Who should you attend to first – the child who has kicked another or the child who has been kicked? Why?

This is a difficult question to answer. Most practitioners would attend to the child who is hurt first, so that first aid can be administered if necessary. This child can then be comforted so he is able to coherently speak to the adult on duty and tell his version of events. Practitioners who see children kicking others are usually quick to call the child over caught kicking and challenge her over her actions. Clearly your professional judgement will impact on whom you attend to first – every situation is different.

Strategies to avoid
◆ Ignore the behaviour.
◆ Kick the child back as punishment – unbelievably I have seen it done!
◆ Shout unnecessarily at the child.

So . . . are you made of the stuff of writers?

27. OUCH! 'She *bit* me!' When children bite

I really value play and give children plenty of opportunities to learn through it. There is one girl in my higher ability group though who has a tendency to bite children during this time and it is really worrying me. What can I do to prevent red teeth marks appearing on all of the children (and potentially me)?

Year 2 teacher

Biting is a difficult behaviour to deal with as it has the potential to cause real pain. Unlike hitting, children have more power in their jaw muscles than in their arms so the damage can be more severe; it can be in the form of:

◆ sore or bleeding fingers/arms;
◆ infections;
◆ unpopularity with playmates.

It is interesting to note that this behaviour can be found in children up to the age of seven even though biting is a more of a recognized behaviour among children between the ages of 18–30 months. Usually it has to be endured until the child (of either sex) is old enough to 'know better'. There are many reasons as to why children bite as presented below.

Activity

Read the 'Details' column provided in the table below and establish which 'Cause' (in bold) relates to which description.

Imitation, Independence, ~~Exploration~~, Stress, Teething, Frustration, Self-Defence, Cause and Effect, Attention

The first one has been done for you. Answers are given at the end of this section.

No. Cause	Details
1 **Exploration**	Infants and toddlers learn through their senses. Tasting or 'mouthing' is a common action to explore a toy which may develop into an accidental bite.
2	Swelling gums are tender and are a discomfort to young children who may relieve this by chewing on something (or someone)!
3	Children like to discover things, e.g. what will happen if I drop this toy or bite this finger?

4	Many children seek attention if they are not potentially the centre of it! Biting, although negative, is a quick way to gain a desired interaction.
5	Control and independence are very important; biting can be used to get what you want in terms of a toy, for example.
6	Children's lives may be fraught with stressful situations, e.g. death, lack of routine, food. Biting may help to relieve tensions.
7	Children like to copy others. A child seeing an adult eating a sausage may use a finger as an alternative!
8	When children cannot find the words they want to express their feelings they will resort to more physical means, e.g. biting.
9	Some children bite because others may have bitten them!

The range of reasons provided above highlights how important it is for practitioners to undertake careful observations of the children to determine the underlying reason as to why they bite (children, that is, not adults!).

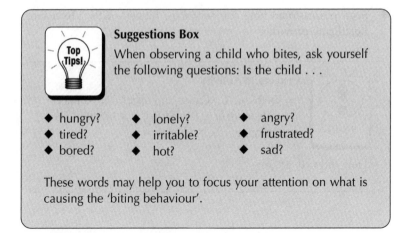

Suggestions Box

When observing a child who bites, ask yourself the following questions: Is the child . . .

◆ hungry? ◆ lonely? ◆ angry?
◆ tired? ◆ irritable? ◆ frustrated?
◆ bored? ◆ hot? ◆ sad?

These words may help you to focus your attention on what is causing the 'biting behaviour'.

It is not enough to just know why a child may bite another; we need to consider strategies to effectively manage and prevent this behaviour.

◆ Always focus your attention on the child who has been bitten first.
◆ Be firm with the biter – tell her you are displeased and that biting is not acceptable.
◆ Provide easier activities for the child if he is frustrated by them.
◆ Provide more toys so there is less fighting.
◆ Decrease the number of children the child has to play near to or with, or the amount of playtime the child has.
◆ Teach the child to say 'No!' if another child does something she does not like.
◆ Closely monitor the child – remove him from an activity if he does bite.
◆ Praise the child when she 'does the right thing' when frustrated.
◆ Talk to the parents/carers – ask them for their support in dealing with the behaviour at home.
◆ Model language to help the child express himself – 'I'm mad! *I* wanted that truck!'
◆ Provide a cuddly toy for children to hug when sad or angry.
◆ Use brief time-out periods if needed.
◆ Provide outdoor energetic activities to let children 'blow off steam'.
◆ Involve the biter in helping to apply first aid to the child who has been bitten.

◆ Seek professional help for persistent biting – GPs, physicians, healthcare provider.

Answers to Activity
2 = Teething, 3 = Cause and effect, 4 = Attention, 5 = Independence, 6 = Stress, 7 = Imitation, 8 = Frustration, 9 = Self-defence

How did you get on?

28. 'Oh! My leg! I think I've *broken* it!' Faking injuries on the playground

Whenever I am on playground duty I have to deal with one particular child who is always faking different injuries. He spends most of his time clutching different parts of his body, crying and complaining of the 'agonizing pain' he is in. How can I help him to be less . . . melodramatic?

Year 4 teacher

Playtime is a great opportunity for most children to get outside and enjoy the benefits of open space, fresh air and physical activity. It is inevitable when 300+ children rush out onto the playground that one or two of them are going to be hurt, either accidentally or deliberately.

Important!
If children regularly come to you stating that they are hurt as a result of the actions of the same individuals then it is most likely that these children are being victimized and bullied. This behaviour must be dealt with swiftly and effectively.

While most children are able to cope with the occasional 'knock', there are those who make out that they are at 'death's door' even though they have only had a ball lightly hit them on the leg! In every school there will be children with a melodramatic disposition which can become irritating and rather draining for practitioners who have to deal with unnecessary sobbing, whining and attention-seeking displays of agony.

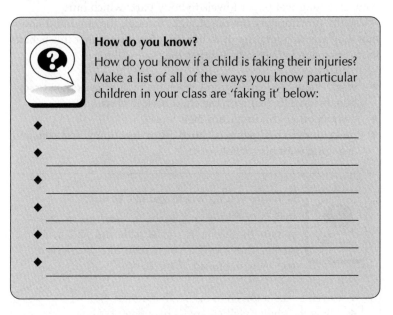

How do you know?

How do you know if a child is faking their injuries? Make a list of all of the ways you know particular children in your class are 'faking it' below:

◆ _____

◆ _____

◆ _____

◆ _____

◆ _____

◆ _____

Children who fake injuries do it for a number of reasons:

◆ attention seeking;
◆ a result of being tired, hot or bothered;
◆ personality trait;
◆ low pain threshold;
◆ assessing gullibility of the practitioner;
◆ avoidance tactics to get out of doing PE or taking a test.

Warning!

Some children who you suspect are faking their injuries may really be injured! Some children suffer from genetic or medical conditions which mean they are more prone to injury than others. Do take care!

Children who fake injuries can be amusing and slightly irritating in the way they try to inform others about the pain they are apparently in. They usually rub their body incessantly, engage in 'dry crying' where no real tears actually appear and/or talk constantly about the pain, clutching wet paper towels to body parts which hurt.

Usually practitioners can see straight through the child and know that they are exaggerating. It is, however, important that this behaviour is managed effectively as it has the potential to:

◆ waste valuable learning and teaching time when other practitioners have to deal with the child back in class;
◆ distract other children from their work;
◆ prevent the child who is 'hurt' from remaining focused and engaging with his schoolwork.

What do you do/would you like to do?
Reflect on the strategies below and put a cross against those which you already use and a tick against those which you would like to adopt as your new improved practice.

◆ Check to see if the child has really hurt herself [   ]
◆ Allow the child to tell you what happened [   ]
◆ Offer the child soothing words to calm him [   ]
◆ Encourage the child to rub the body part which is hurting [   ]
◆ Ask a child to go and get the hurt child a 'magic' wet paper towel (they work wonders!) [   ]
◆ Make a joke out of it, e.g. 'If your (leg) drops off in the next five minutes then tell me and I will sew it back on for you!' [   ]
◆ Ask the child to sit out for five minutes to calm down. Go back to her in a while to see if she is okay [   ]
◆ Ask the child to find a friend to look after him [   ]
◆ Sprinkle some imaginary 'magic healing dust' over her [   ]
◆ Distract the child by giving him a special job to do, e.g. blow the whistle or go in to give a message to another practitioner [   ]
◆ Strategically ignore whingeing and 'acting' [   ]
◆ Encourage the child to be brave [   ]
◆ Use bravery stickers where appropriate [   ]

Top Tip!

Distraction is the best way to prevent children who fake injuries interfering with valuable learning and teaching time. Engaging them in stimulating, interactive activities will soon make them forget that their foot 'apparently' hurts!

29. *Hock Toth!* Spitting in the playground

A rather antisocial game is being played by some of my class at the moment. They like to see how far they can spit from a line in the playground! Although a number of children and parents have complained about this game, many continue to play it and I really feel as if I need to do something to stop this once and for all. What would you suggest?

Year 5 teacher

Spitting, like kicking and biting, is a very unpleasant behaviour and children should be made aware right from the start that this is an unacceptable thing to do, irrespective of whether the children think it is a game or not. Being spat on is terribly unpleasant and most probably will make some readers cringe at the thought of it actually happening.

Scenario

A child is caught spitting while on the playground. Consider the following:

1. Why are they doing it?
2. What can be done to stop them from doing it?

Reflect on your ideas as you engage with the rest of this section.

Children who spit either do it on their own for their own reason or pleasure or spit at other children. It is more of an observed behaviour in boys rather than girls as it considered by some as a 'manly' action (like cowboys chewing/spitting tobacco). It is not specific to one particular key stage and is likely to continue as a 'regular' behaviour into their teens unless it is effectively managed at an early years/primary level. But first we need to establish potential causes as to why children spit. These include the child:

◆ playing a game – 'Pooh Spits' (a variation on 'Pooh Sticks');
◆ imitating others – parents who chew tobacco, footballers;
◆ having a medical condition;

- trying to act tough in front of her peers;
- having a phlegmy cough – trying to clear throat;
- swallowing a bug by accident;
- eating or drinking something he does not like;
- being frustrated by another child – uses spitting as a way to get what he wants or to stop others from playing with him/his toys;
- being intrigued by the bodily function;
- seeking attention;
- defending herself from others;
- is about to vomit;
- talking too fast – accidental spray of saliva on another child.

Most people do not like others spitting because it usually lands on the floor where people are walking, or on clothing or shoes. Nobody likes to have to wipe saliva off themselves and so children need be made aware of the feelings of others before they consider opening their mouth to spit with others around them.

So . . . how would you go about managing this behaviour? Would you:

- inform the child that spitting is not acceptable?
- ask the child why she is spitting?
- speak to parents and carers – is this behaviour occurring at home?
- suggest a visit to the local GP if the behaviour continues?
- make children aware of why it is unpleasant for others to see and hear other children spitting?
- identify reasons as to when it is right/wrong to spit?
- talk to the children about the need for saliva – hydration of the body and the breaking down of foods?
- talk to the children about germs and diseases?
- encourage the children to go to the toilet and use the sink/lavatory to clear their throat if they need to?

Controversial Case Study

A practitioner in Foundation Two found a number of children had begun to spit at her when they were asked to engage in activities they did not want to be involved in. One day she introduced the children to Max, a sock puppet, who was being stubborn and did not want to join in with the table top activities. The practitioner encouraged the children to try to convince Max with reasons as to why he should undertake the activities on offer. Max, clearly frustrated, opened his mouth and 'spat' on all the children (water was pumped out of a tube connected to a bottle in the practitioner's pocket). The children screamed out in horror – one child stood up, smacked the puppet right across the head, saying he was '. . . very naughty!'

'But some of you do that to me,' said the practitioner.

All of the children fell silent.

The message had finally sunk in – do not spit on others because it is not nice!

Would you do this to your children – why / why not?

30. Trying to keep an eye on all of them: Children and the boundaries of the playground

Why do children always have to push the physical boundaries when they are on the playground? Whenever I am on duty children are forever going behind the bike shed, around the tall fence, over the low flowerbeds and onto the field even though they know they are not allowed to. What can I do when there seems to be 200+ children to keep in check?

Year 2 Teaching Assistant

Most practitioners, irrespective of how many years' experience they have had, find playtime a challenge due to the large number of children all running around and shouting at the same time! While it is impossible to keep an eye on every child, it is important for practitioners to know they are all in the same place, i.e. the parameters or boundaries of the playground.

Reflective questions

◆ Do children know where the boundaries of the playground are in your school/setting?
◆ How do they know these boundaries?
◆ Are there any features in and around the playground which children could hide behind?
◆ What effect do these have on the potential health and safety of the children?

Playgrounds are usually large, open, tarmacked spaces and most children know that where the tarmac ends is where the playground ends. However, low walls, pathways, high wire fences, bike sheds, wooden shacks, gates, benches, flowerbeds and other features including the ever-popular field are places where children might play in, on, around or behind, and this can cause issues when you blow the whistle and 15 children fail to line up with their rest of the class!

Important to remember! The shape of the school/setting may provide unusual places for children to play and hide in where practitioners cannot see them. Whether in Foundation or Key Stage 1/2 children will find these places and play in them unless those on duty 'move them on'. So why do children like to push the boundaries of the playground? Possible reasons include:

◆ excitement;
◆ a test to see how far they can push the boundaries with those on duty;
◆ unaware features are 'out of bounds';
◆ seeking attention;
◆ genuine mistake – children 'carried away' with their game;
◆ place for privacy – quiet chat, space to be alone from others, a place for a quick kiss (!);
◆ part of the game – need spaces to hide from others (they are playing Hide and Seek after all!);
◆ playground too small for older children – need more space;
◆ playground too big for younger children – need to get away from 'herds of big kids'.

What do you do?

How do you keep children within the boundaries of the playground during playtime? Reflect on the strategies suggested below, indicating which ones you use (A), those which you would not use (B) and those you would like to use (C):

◆ Mark boundaries with chalk on floor [   ]
◆ Use cones and markers to corner off areas where children should not go [   ]
◆ Call for children to come from features they should not be behind [   ]
◆ Use playground monitors (older children) to monitor areas [   ]
◆ Position yourself so you can keep an eye on the 'hot spots' of the playground [   ]
◆ Tape off areas in which the children are not allowed to play [   ]
◆ Strategically ignore children who step over the boundaries [   ]
◆ Make 'boundary breakers' walk with you around the playground for a little while [   ]
◆ Use other members of staff to deal with issues [   ]
◆ Use your whistle to call children back onto the playground [   ]
◆ Provide areas for privacy [   ]

Clearly children will push the boundaries unless they know where they can and cannot play. Children need to not only be told where the boundaries are but also be physically shown. Ways this can be achieved include:

◆ talking to the whole school about the playground boundaries;
◆ using Over Head Transparencies (OHTs)/digital images to indicate boundaries;
◆ physically walk small groups/whole classes around the boundary edge.

Most importantly, children need to know why these boundaries exist.

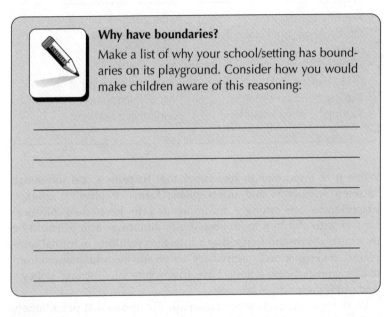

Why have boundaries?
Make a list of why your school/setting has boundaries on its playground. Consider how you would make children aware of this reasoning:

But what do you do if you continuously find children overstepping the boundaries?
Well . . . that's for you to decide!

31. 'Hold my hand!' Children who seek physical contact from practitioners

A new pupil has recently arrived in our class and is settling in quite well. I am, however, a little worried about her constant need for physical contact from me – she is forever trying to hold hands and kiss and stroke me! What can/should I do to manage this?

Year 1 teacher

Virtually all children (and adults) like physical contact from other people, be it from their family and/or friends. This contact can come in a variety of forms and be used for a number of different reasons as highlighted overleaf:

Forms of contact	Reasons
Holding hands	Offer comfort
Stroking hair, arms, face, legs	Sign of friendship
or back	Sign of affection
Hugging	Gain attention
Cuddling	Form of communication
Placing hand on shoulder	'Nice' thing to do
Resting head on shoulder	Confidence booster

While it is important to remember that there is a real difference between acceptable and unacceptable forms of physical contact, practitioners are strongly recommended to keep their physical contact with children to an absolute minimum as actions could be misconstrued by children/other adults thus resulting in formal complaints, investigations, disciplinary action and even suspension from teaching posts. Some schools have an absolute 'no touching' policy – find out if your school has one.

Working in the early years automatically means that practitioners will have lots of physical contact with young children due to the nature of the work they are engaged in. While this is accepted by most, practitioners should still be aware of the need to be careful, particularly if they have a naturally 'touchy feely' nature.

Children may seek physical contact from practitioners for a number of additional reasons:

◆ wants to be loved;
◆ used to a lot of contact with parents/carers at home;
◆ it is the 'norm' – children in France, for example, greet each other with kisses on both cheeks;
◆ reassurance;
◆ feeling upset or lonely;
◆ curiosity – wants to know how skin/hair feels;
◆ just a game – the practitioner is 'the prize';
◆ child has 'feelings' for the practitioner;
◆ child feels safe with the practitioner.

With these reasons in mind practitioners are better placed to use strategies to manage this behaviour. Possible strategies include:

◆ directing the child to an activity;
◆ making an excuse – your hand is getting a little hot!;
◆ having objects in your hand – pens, paper – to prevent you from holding theirs;
◆ having a teddy the children can use for emotional support;
◆ encouraging friends to offer physical support for others if appropriate.

To prevent this behaviour from occurring all the children in your class need to understand that it is not appropriate for you to touch them as you are there to teach them. Establish clear and suitable boundaries so that every child knows what is acceptable.

Remember! Never touch a child while you are alone with them. It should always be in the open and in public.

Reflection questions
◆ What is acceptable/unacceptable physical contact with children in your school?
◆ How do you know?

Physical contact with children is a difficult and sensitive topic of discussion because one person's views may totally contradict another's. Is it really acceptable to hold a child's hand as you lead your class into assembly?

For some practitioners the gender and the age of the child impacts on how they would deal with this incident. While it is a tricky situation, most adults instinctively want to comfort children who are upset. Would you 'hold back' and thus appear unsympathetic and distant, or offer lots of support which in the eyes of some would make you a 'mother/father figure'? Clearly it is down to one's own professional judgement.

Scenario

A child has fallen over and is clearly distressed as they have cut their knee. The child seeks some physical contact from you – what do you do?

Discuss your responses with other colleagues in your school. Consider if/how your actions would change if the child were:

a) a boy;
b) a girl;
c) in Early Years Foundation Stage;
d) in Key Stage 1;
e) in Key Stage 2.

Think about it!

Children may think that physical contact is somehow 'wrong' if practitioners flinch or pull themselves away from them. Children need to understand why practitioners cannot behave in this way, otherwise this could have an adverse effect on the child's ability to have effective relationships with other people in later life.

32. 'Just *stop* it, will you?' The child who deliberately interferes with others' game play

Whenever my class goes out to play there is one child who seems to take great delight in deliberately interfering with other children's games. He will kick the football way from the pitch, 'tick' children without knowing what team he is supposed to be on, and generally irritate those around him to the point when I receive lots of complaints about his behaviour. What am I to do about this?

Year 2 teacher

Children who set out to ruin the fun of other children on the playground make their peers' and practitioners' lives a bit of a misery, particularly when they have been explicitly told not to continue behaving in that manner for the fourth time in a row!

Observation Time!

Take a few moments during one playtime to observe one or two children (they do not necessarily have to be in your class) who regularly interfere with other children's game play. Make a note of the following:

◆ The children involved in the incident.
◆ The time at which it took place.
◆ What the child was doing which was causing a disruption.
◆ Why the child was being a nuisance.
◆ What the other children did to manage the behaviour of the child.
◆ What the practitioner on duty did to support the children involved.
◆ How effective the children's and practitioner's actions were.

Undertake another observation of the children again a couple of days later – how do the observations compare?

As most playtimes last only 15 minutes it is important that children are able to play and have fun without having to deal with unnecessary and irritating distractions and interference from others. So why do some children interfere with other children's game play?

Yes or No?

Take a look at the reasons below and circle the 'Y' if you agree with them or circle the 'N' if you do not think they support reasoning as to why children may interfere with others' game play:

Child is bored.	Child wants to play with others but does not have the social skills to ask if they can join in.	Child wants one of their parents/ carers.	Child likes to aggravate others.
Y N	Y N	Y N	Y N

Child is seeking atten- tion.	Child does not know how to play with others.	Child has short attention span and needs to engage in lots of different activities.	Child does not have many friends.
Y N	Y N	Y N	Y N

Most children who interfere with other children's game play are either seeking attention, simply do not know how to ask others if they can play or know how to play the game being played. There are many management strategies practitioners can put into place and so those reading this should be selective in which strategies they would like to adopt as their own practice:

◆ Teach children to either ignore the child disturbing them or use their outstretched hand to 'stop' them.
◆ Use your 'practitioner glare'.
◆ Use time out.
◆ Do listen to 'both sides of the story' before you act.

◆ Talk to the child about her behaviour – how could she change it?
◆ Teach the child a game he can play on his own.
◆ Support the child in asking others if she can join in their play.
◆ Ensure the children being irritated do not take 'matters into their own hands' by using physical measures.
◆ Provide lots of playground resources so children are kept occupied.
◆ Play games with the child and, as others begin to watch and want to get involved, allow others to seamlessly take your place.

To prevent this behaviour becoming a real issue schools and practitioners should ensure that systems and approaches are in place to combat 'interfering' behaviours:

◆ Create and share playground rules with the children.
◆ Display these around the playground so children are constantly made aware of them.
◆ Have a sequence of sanctions available for persistent 'offenders'.
◆ Use PSHCE and circle time opportunities to explore situations and scenarios which occur on the playground.
◆ Encourage older children in the school to play with children who need to be engaged in productive play.

 Top Tip!
Undertaking observations of children who regularly interfere with other children's game play helps to build an evidence base of information which can be shared with parents/carers and staff members to help formulate an effective plan of action/IEP.

5 | 'Testing' behaviours

33. The 'Bully' and the 'Bullied': Children and bullying at school

In my class there are two children who are forever causing me stress and anxiety. One of them is clearly bullying the other and it is really noticeable in the way that they both act towards each other and how it is affecting their work. I regularly have to speak to both parents about this issue – they are as concerned about this as I am. What is the best approach to managing this?

Year 3 teacher

Nearly every child (and adult) is bullied at one time or another in their life. It may not be just by their peers but by siblings or even adults including practitioners. With bullying a high-priority area of educational and public concern (particularly racist bullying), schools are continuously seeking new and effective ways to manage 'bullies' and support the 'bullied'.

Defining the terms

What do we actually mean by the term 'bully' and those children who are 'bullied'? Use the grid below to record your thoughts in relation to the kinds of behaviours they both exhibit, feelings they experience and the reasons as to why they are either the bully or the bullied.

The bully   *The bullied*

_____   _____

_____   _____

_____   _____

_____   _____

_____   _____

_____   _____

_____   _____

_____   _____

_____   _____

Refer to the following websites to compare your responses and thinking:

- www.bullying.co.uk;
- www.antibullying.net;
- www.childline.org.uk
- www.nspcc.org.uk/kidszone

Bullying affects children in many different ways. These include feelings of being alone, scared, sad, worried or embarrassed. Many children experience levels of unnecessary stress which can lead to depression, eating disorders and even suicide.

Important! Bullies take the fun out of school. Bullying bothers everyone – not just the child who is being bullied. Nobody likes a bully and nobody deserves to be bullied. Children should always seek help to sort out the situation. But this is easier said than done.

What would you do?

You suspect that a child in your class is being bullied. They are withdrawn, have lost weight and hate coming to school. You have invited the child to come and speak to you but the child refuses and 'shuts down' when you mention the word 'bullying'. Consider what you would do to manage this situation. Make a note of your ideas below and reflect on the strategies suggested in the remainder of this section.

Many children who are being bullied are frightened that if they tell an adult then the bully will come back after them, and what started out as name-calling and teasing develops into threatening behaviour, damage to their belongings or physical violence. So how should practitioners deal with this?

◆ If the child does not feel comfortable talking to you then encourage them to speak to their parents/carers, friends, siblings or another adult in school, e.g. a TA or a midday supervisor. *Childline* has a free number children can call 24 hours a day (0800 1111).

◆ Encourage the children to write a note or email you. Texting is another option if the child does not like face-to-face discussions.

Children need strategies and advice to help them if they are being bullied.

Act brave – hold your head up high and smile!	Ignore the bully – this will rob her of her fun of getting a reaction from you.	Stand up for yourself – use verbal rather than physical means to stop him.
Be a buddy to someone you believe or know is being bullied.	Always let someone know you are being bullied.	Read books about bullying to find out how others have dealt with it.

A number of recommendations/pieces of advice are provided below which practitioners are encouraged to share with children when talking about bullying in PHSCE and circle time sessions:

◆ Try to avoid being alone in places where you know the bully is likely to pick on you.
◆ Keep a diary log of what is happening – note dates, times and places.
◆ Please do not hit the bully back (however tempting!).
◆ Please avoid missing school.
◆ If you are an 'onlooker' (someone who watches others being bullied), then you should tell an adult.

While most of this discussion has focused on the 'bullied' we should also consider appropriate support for the 'bully'. Strategies include:

◆ providing individual counselling sessions;
◆ teaching children to play and work effectively with others;
◆ helping children to form friendships;
◆ building their self-esteem;
◆ praising them when they are kind to others;
◆ using parental partnerships to support/implement strategies;
◆ believing that they *can* change.

34. Moody Two Shoes! Moody children – normal or not?

There is one child in my class who is an extremely moody individual. She can be the most wonderful, well-behaved and intelligent child one moment and then be angry, depressed and irritable the next. This rather erratic behaviour makes it difficult for her to work with and make friends with the other children as they never know what she is going to be like! How can I help manage her difficult mood swings?

Year 5 teacher

Most adults working with young people would say that children have the potential to be erratic, moody and difficult. However, they are not as erratic, moody and difficult as their reputation would have us believe – in fact this is something of a cultural myth.

Naturally there are times when everyone, irrespective of age or sex, experiences some sort of 'mood swing' which is usually dependent on a number of factors including the weather, the amount of sleep the person has had, whether they have had an argument with someone or are just having 'one of those days'.

The Mood factor!
Consider what other factors may potentially influence children's mood swings. Please list them below:

◆ _____   _____

◆ _____   _____

◆ _____   _____

◆ _____   _____

◆ _____   _____

◆ _____   _____

◆ _____   _____

By the side of each factor please note the name of a child in your class who you think/know becomes moody as a result of each of these factors.

However, we need to be clear that we are not talking about children who seem grumpy and 'blue' for a little while and then become their normal cheery self. Instead it seems that the Year 5 teacher is describing a child who has quite severe mood swings. Establishing the causes of this will help practitioners to select appropriate strategies to manage these mood swings. Possible causes of this behaviour include:

◆ Clinical depression – this is unlikely unless the child is suffering from the aftermath of a seriously traumatic incident.
◆ Immaturity – inability to cope with and manage their own feelings.
◆ Hormones – some girls and boys may have reached puberty at an early age.

Remember, oh do remember!

Lots of children are vulnerable to getting 'bumped' into a bad mood and find it harder than others to climb out of their slump – this is a very normal tendency to have!

Clearly managing this behaviour is important as it has the potential to affect learning and teaching in the classroom as practitioners have to deal with 'stroppy' children who have either fallen out with their friends or refuse to engage with the activities set for them to complete. Here are some basic approaches for practitioners to try:

Approach	Description
Nurture	Children who are prone to mood swings need extra attention from their parents/carers and practitioners to help them overcome their low feelings. Ensure quality one-to-one opportunities are planned (individual reading, chat at dinnertime, working next to them during a lesson) to offer support, advice and help as and where necessary.

Reflection	Encourage children to think about the 'good times' or good feelings they have experienced. Moody children need to build up a positive emotional memory to help sooth themselves when life becomes a challenge.
Management	Try to ensure moody children's lives are as stress-free as possible. Ensure there are enough breaks during the day and that you do not have unreasonable expectations of them.
Other working adults	Ask work colleagues to observe you in the classroom with the child – is there anything they spot which triggers off his moodiness?
Health	Work with the school cooks and parents/carers to ensure the child is getting a balanced diet. Consider the effects food allergies may be having on the child's moods.

But what should practitioners and children do when they are faced with a moody child? Strategies include:

◆ Give the child some time alone – allow her to sit in a corner away from the other children.
◆ Encourage the other children in class to give the moody child 'some space'.
◆ Never refer to the child as 'moody' (I am only using this term to define the type of child I am talking about!).
◆ Allow the child to rejoin working groups when he is calm and ready to return.
◆ Empathize with the child.
◆ Ensure the child does not take out her feelings on either you or the other children in class – remind her it is not your fault she is feeling the way she is (unless you are the direct cause of it).
◆ Try to distract the child with something nice, interesting or unusual.

35. 'Why don't you just f*** off!'
Swearing in the classroom

*It is not often I am lost for words (after all, I am a teacher!), but I recently had a child in my nurture group turn and tell me to '. . . go and f*** myself'! I just stood there, absolutely flabbergasted! In my day, if I had done that to my teacher, I probably would have not been able to sit down for a week! How can I prevent this language from being used in the classroom, especially by this child?*

Year 4 teacher

Hearing children swear can be quite shocking, even more so when the swearing is directed at you. It signals a loss of innocence in the child even though there are people who believe swear words to be just a heightened form of verbal emotional expression and are not really 'offensive'. Your views on this behaviour will directly impact the way you attempt to manage it.

Reflection time!
- How do you feel when you hear children swearing?
- What age of children have you heard swearing?
- In what contexts have you heard children swearing?
- How do you attempt to manage this behaviour?

Most adults are very concerned about children they work with who swear – if you were not concerned about it then you would not be reading this! Children of all ages have been known to swear, yet many practitioners question how children get to know these words and why they use them. Possible reasons include:

How they get to hear/know swear words	Why they use swear words
◆ Heard and used at home by parents/carers and wider family. ◆ Taught to use it by rebellious siblings. ◆ Accidental use of it by practitioner. ◆ Used by characters in reading book – Harry Potter. ◆ Heard on TV, in song lyrics, on radio, in magazines, on advertisements. ◆ Peers use it to make them appear 'cool'.	◆ Feel like a grown up. ◆ Seek attention. ◆ Prove their independence. ◆ Gain peer acceptance. ◆ Mimic what they see or hear in the media. ◆ They do not know the right words to express themselves fully. ◆ Deliberately want to offend or verbally assault others.

Top Tip!

Ensure any music or videos/DVDs children bring into school are lyrically and age appropriate. No music should be played with a parental advisory sign indicating explicit content, nor should films/ programmes be viewed by the children which are rated 12A or above.

It is important to remember that some children swear as a result of neurological problems or a language disorder known as Tourette's Syndrome.

Find Out!

What do you know about Tourette's? Take a few moments to any visit three websites dedicated to this syndrome. Highlight key points and share this information with your colleagues. Alternatively have a look at the Tourette's section in Chapter 9 (pages 228–231)!

While swearing is offensive we should remember that we as adults swear, even though we may not do it in public. Those children who swear regularly have not been taught to swear responsibly – this is an important topic of discussion to have with them on a one-to-one basis.

Managing this behaviour effectively takes a certain level of skill and preparation. The following do's and don'ts are a guide for support:

Do	Don't
◆ Keep calm. ◆ Maintain eye contact. ◆ Clearly state that you are displeased with their choice of vocabulary. ◆ Use a quiet but firm tone of voice. ◆ Offer alternative words they could use, e.g. drat, darn, gee whiz, golly. ◆ Use role play scenarios to model appropriate ways to express anger and frustration. ◆ Praise children when they use suitable language to express themselves.	◆ Automatically give a shocked response. ◆ Swear back at the child. ◆ Laugh at their outburst. ◆ Slap a child. ◆ Wash their mouth out with soap and water. ◆ Say to them 'What did you say?' as they will most probably say it again! ◆ Get into a lengthy debate about inappropriate forms of language.

Activity

Use a highlighter pen and indicate a couple of strategies above which you intend to adopt as your own practice. Set a date by the side of each strategy by when you will review the effectiveness of these strategies.

If swearing is an issue for your class it is important to use PHSCE and circle time opportunities to talk about the differences between formal and informal language, and what can be said in different situations and to different audiences.

36. 'Miss, is *that* right?' Children who need constant reassurance

I work with a boy who drives me to distraction! He needs to be constantly reassured that what he is doing is right! Every word, every sum – anything he does has to be checked over before he adds a little more to his work. I am becoming fed up of saying, 'Yes, that's right' all the time! What can I do about this?

Year 3 teaching assistant

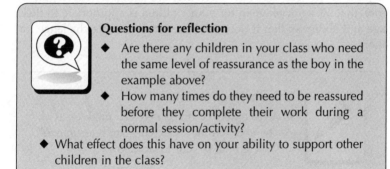

Questions for reflection

◆ Are there any children in your class who need the same level of reassurance as the boy in the example above?

◆ How many times do they need to be reassured before they complete their work during a normal session/activity?

◆ What effect does this have on your ability to support other children in the class?

Children who seek reassurance in what they do can be extremely frustrating and draining for practitioners to manage as it is usually required every few seconds/minutes, and the child who seeks it will not usually make any further progress in their work unless they know they are 'doing right'.

Top Tips!

◆ Please avoid losing your temper with these children – most already have low self-esteem.

◆ Empathize with them – educational learning can be a struggle for some.

◆ Remind yourself when you last had to learn something difficult, or sit a test, or write a complicated essay. We all need reassurance at times from others to check that we are doing okay.

◆ Talk to parents/carers about their child – do they have to offer lots of reassurance at home?

Seeking reassurance is a clear sign that children are uncomfortable, unclear or nervous about the work they are doing. Do ensure, therefore, that all work planned for your children is appropriate to their age and ability so that it does not pose too much of a challenge for them.

Reflecting on reasoning

◆ What other reasoning can you think of as to why children may seek constant reassurance? Make a note of your ideas below:

_____

_____

_____

_____

_____

_____

_____

Children of any age who are taught that it is 'wrong to make mistakes' are certain to develop this needy behaviour. Parents/carers and practitioners who expect children to get everything right first time put children under tremendous and unnecessary pressure.

Fact: We all make mistakes. Most of us are able to learn from these mistakes and move forwards from these experiences in a positive way. Children who are made to feel ashamed of their misunderstandings will inevitably seek constant reassurance so they do not have to experience feelings of sadness, embarrassment and apprehension that they have been subjected to previously.

Activity

Talk to colleagues in your school and, if possible, undertake some observations of them working with children. Use the chart below to record how they promote a 'making mistakes is fine!' atmosphere for the children to work in.

How making mistakes is okay!

There are a number of ways in which practitioners will be able to spot children who need constant reassurance:

♦ Always asking if their work is okay.
♦ Asking peers to check their work for them.
♦ Moving from adult to adult in the classroom to check their work.
♦ Looking at other children's work.
♦ Catching your eye for reassurance.
♦ Overreliance on a dictionary or a calculator for checking spellings and answers.

To manage this behaviour there are a range of strategies and approaches to adopt and avoid:

Always	Avoid
♦ Offer children limited support. ♦ Encourage children to 'have a go'. ♦ Praise children for any attempts they have made on their work. ♦ Set children little targets to achieve. ♦ Regularly assess how children are progressing. ♦ Suggest children leave a gap in their work if they are unsure about something and come back to it later. ♦ Encourage children to use support strategies around the classroom – displays, alphabet lines. ♦ Offer lots of verbal/written feedback to make them feel good about themselves. ♦ Build up work expectations over time. ♦ Display children's work.	♦ Doing the work for them. ♦ Spending too much time with them. ♦ Sitting next to them for the whole lesson as they will become very dependent on you. ♦ Using more able children to support children who need constant reassurance – they will become frustrated by their behaviour. ♦ Leaving children on their own for the whole lesson – they will not make any progress if you do this. ♦ Encouraging children to come to you – ask them to put their hand up and wait for you rather then getting out of their seat all the time.

37. *Scribble de scribble!* The child who draws on other children's work

I find it difficult to sit a particular boy near to anyone in my class because he has a tendency to scribble all over their work, be it art, literacy or geography-based. He has ruined some great work and I am embarrassed when I have to explain at parents evening why some children have scribble marks in their workbooks. What can I do about this?

Year 2 teacher

We have all had children come to us with what looks like early years mark making (early writing) all over their work even though they may be in upper Key Stage 2! It is deeply upsetting for children to have their hard work ruined by the actions of someone who clearly has low self-esteem and does not feel that their work is, or ever can be, of the same standard as that of others.

What would you do?

Consider what your feelings and actions would be if you were presented with a wonderful drawing a child had done which was scribbled over in black felt tip pen by another child. Make a note of how you would react to the situation below:

_____

_____

_____

_____

_____

_____

While getting angry and shouting at the 'scribbler' would be a natural and deserved reaction, verbally chastising them is not the most appropriate way to effectively manage the behaviour. However, we need to be aware of other reasons as to why children will do this before we can select the best way to manage the behaviour. These include:

1. Deliberate attention seeking – thinks it is 'a bit of fun'.
2. Child is 'getting back' at a peer for something they may have done or said to them.
3. Poor social skills.
4. Lack of empathy with others.
5. Actually wanted to collaborate with others.
6. Accidental slippage (unlikely if the marks cover the work!).

In response to these reasons above, practitioners may consider using the following strategies:

Reason No.	Strategies
1	Focus your attention on the child whose work has been scribbled on.
2	Use time out or send the 'scribbler' to another class.
3	Talk to the children together during play/dinnertime to resolve the situation.
4	Inform parents/carers about the incident so they can follow up issues at home.
5	Provide close supervision during tasks set – talk to the child about what she is are doing to help her stay focused.
6	Teach children how to talk to others about their work.
7	Talk to the child about the feelings of those whose work he has scribbled on.
8	Pretend to scribble on his work (ensure pen lid is actually on) – how would he feel if you had really done it?
9	Clearly state whether children are able to collaborate or not on work set.
10	Provide a balance of individual, paired and group work.
11	Ensure suitable space is provided for children to work in.
12	Provide 'cardboard booths' (card folded in three) for children to work in.

Activity
Use a highlighter pen and indicate which strategies you intend to adopt as your own practice. Review them after you have to deal with a scribbling incident – how effective were they in helping you manage the situation?

Warning! Children who scribble on other children's work are more likely to do it when they are upset, stressed, rushed or frustrated. To prevent these feelings being 'expressed' on others' work practitioners should:

◆ adapt work in terms of content, scope and the amount where appropriate;
◆ provide plenty of time for children to complete their work and give warnings as to when they need to finish by;
◆ provide support either from practitioners or peers if a child is struggling (where appropriate);
◆ encourage children to vent their feelings in other ways, e.g. stress ball, vigorous running outside, time out;
◆ ensure the children know the work is not a 'competition', they should do the best they can.

Good practice relating to managing this behaviour is presented in the following strategies:

◆ Do remain calm.
◆ Empathize with the child whose work has been scribbled on.
◆ Ensure all children know that scribbling on others' work is not acceptable.
◆ Have appropriate sanctions in place to punish 'scribblers'.
◆ Work to raise the self-esteem of 'scribblers'.
◆ If time allows work with children to produce a new piece of work.
◆ Always get 'scribblers' to sincerely apologize for their actions.

38. Having an accident: Children who soil themselves

I have a child who has just recently started to have a number of 'toilet accidents' in class. While I recognize this is not uncommon in young children, the child in my class is nine years old and, as a result, is being teased a great deal by the other children. Why has this just started and what can I do to prevent it happening?

Year 4 teacher

Most practitioners, if asked, would say that most children soil themselves during the early years of their schooling. 'Accidents' at this age do happen and all early years settings have systems in place to manage incidences in a calm and effective manner. Practitioners in Key Stage 1 may encounter the odd incident, but by the time children enter Year 2 these accidents are of rare occurrence. In Key Stage 2 most practitioners would be extremely surprised if a child in their class soiled themselves. But it does happen, irrespective of their age or sex.

What are the issues?

Knowing the issues relating to incidents involving children who have soiled themselves will allow practitioners to reflect on the difficult circumstances it puts practitioners, the child who has soiled herself and the rest of the class in.

Make a list of the issues this behaviour would cause in the classroom and the potential outcomes of these – an example has been done for you:

◆ Unpleasant smell in classroom – class unable to settle and continue with their work.

◆ _____

◆ _____

◆ _____

◆ _____

◆ _____

Clearly there are a number of reasons as to why this behaviour occurs and practitioners need to understand and appreciate these. Reasons include:

1. Child has a medical condition – retention issues.
2. Child is attention seeking.
3. An indication of sudden illness.
4. Child forgot to 'go' – engrossed in activities.
5. Child is unfortunately 'caught short' – did not get to the toilet in time.
6. Child passed wind and 'followed through'.
7. Child did it for a dare.
8. A reaction to some deeply traumatic issues at home.
9. Child is tired or exhausted.
10. Child is suddenly shocked by a noise.
11. Child has a fear of toilets used by lots of other children – unclean, smelly.

Which are 'key'?

Reflect on the reasons identified above and indicate which reasons are 'key' to identifying the common causes as to why children may soil themselves by using a highlighter pen. Compare your responses to the answers given at the end of this section.

Strategies to manage this behaviour work on different levels which we will explore in turn:

Dealing with the incident

◆ Remain calm.
◆ Talk quietly to the child, asking him to step into the toilet area and remove his soiled clothing (if appropriate).
◆ Ask other practitioners to take charge of the class, if appropriate. If not, ask them to assist the child.

Take care! Physical contact with children is prohibited – ensure you speak to your headteacher as the child may have to be sent home.

◆ Avoid shouting at the child and drawing attention to her and the issue.
◆ Refocus the rest of the class back onto their work.

Top Tip!
Practitioners in all classes should have to hand a labelled box in their classroom containing the following:

◆ carrier bags;
◆ wet wipes;
◆ plastic gloves;
◆ disinfectant spray;
◆ air freshener;
◆ cloths;
◆ a spare set of both boy's and girl's clothing including underwear and socks.

This should be locked away in a cupboard but is there to help practitioners to manage incidents if and when they occur in a speedy and positive way.

But what if you did not have any other practitioners in the classroom or the rest of the class would not refocus? Reflect on the ideas in the suggestions box below:

Suggestions Box
Other practitioners: Ask a child from your class to get a practitioner from another class to help or pass a message to the school administrator/head-teacher asking for support.
Class: Sensitively discuss the issue with the class, keeping details to a minimum. Ensure you play the severity of the incident down, asking the class to be 'grown up' and continue with their work. Stress the importance of the rest of the class not teasing the child over the incident afterwards.

After the incident:

◆ Direct the child back to his work.

◆ Offer emotional support if necessary.

◆ Talk about why the child did it, out of the earshot of others.

◆ Empathize with her but state that her behaviour is inappropriate/unacceptable.

◆ Make a written note of when the incident happened.

◆ Inform parents/carers.

Oh . . . and one final idea . . . *open the windows*!

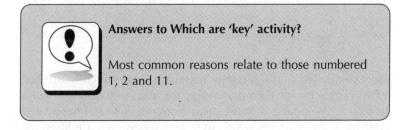

Answers to Which are 'key' activity?

Most common reasons relate to those numbered 1, 2 and 11.

39. 'Move *back*! Move *away* from me!' Children who invade others' personal space

There is one child in my class who does not seem to understand the concept of 'personal space'. She is forever sitting too closely to others, trying to squeeze into tiny gaps between people and using her arms and legs to interfere and disrupt her peers. What can I do to teach this girl about the need for one's own personal space?

Year 1 teacher

Everyone needs their own personal space – both adult and child. If someone sits too closely next to us on the bus or is stood right behind us in a queue we begin to feel . . . well, how *do* we feel?

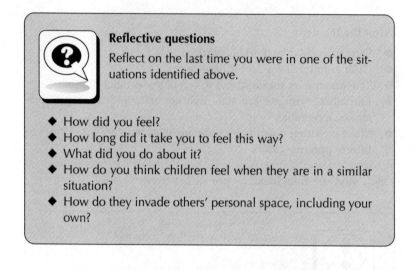

Reflective questions

Reflect on the last time you were in one of the situations identified above.

◆ How did you feel?
◆ How long did it take you to feel this way?
◆ What did you do about it?
◆ How do you think children feel when they are in a similar situation?
◆ How do they invade others' personal space, including your own?

Most people feel uncomfortable, apprehensive and slightly irritated when people invade their personal space, and immediately attempt to seek some suitable distance away from others to feel happy and content in the space in which they find themselves. Children are exactly the same and are appreciative of their 'own space' in school, be it sat on the carpet, at a table or outside on the playground.

Activity

Make a list of all the different occasions during the school day in which children may invade other children's personal space. Use the table provided below to collect your thoughts and ideas. A few examples have been done to support you.

		Lining up to go out to play.
	Queuing up for school dinners.	
Washing hands before going for dinner.		

While it is clear there are a number of occasions when children will resent invasion of their personal space, we need some clarity as to why some children are intent on stepping into each other's personal space:

◆ Child has no concept of personal space.
◆ Child likes physical closeness with others.
◆ Child is insecure or upset.
◆ Child is seeking attention, deliberately trying to irritate others to generate a reaction.
◆ Child is apprehensive about others nearby – being bullied or hurt by others perhaps.

By being mindful of these reasons practitioners are in a better position to utilize the best strategies to manage this behaviour. Children whose personal space is being invaded are quick to exhibit any of the following behaviours:

◆ Push others away;   ◆ Attempt to wriggle away;
◆ Kick others;   ◆ Constantly move about;
◆ Punch others;   ◆ Slap others;
◆ Tell their practitioner;   ◆ Get verbally abusive.
◆ Run away;

While it is understandable why these children will use these strategies, it is important for us to ensure children are taught that physical retaliation is not acceptable – most of the above are strategies we should *avoid* encouraging children to use to deal with the situation. So what strategies are available for us to advocate?

Case study

One morning a Year 3 teacher carefully placed 30 small carpet sample squares given to the school by a parent on the carpeted area. When the children came into class they are asked to sit on a carpet square away from their friends. Issues with personal space suddenly stopped! The children liked the carpet squares so much that 'Carpet Monitors' were established to set out/collect the squares on a daily basis.

On the downside, however, issues became apparent when the girls began to argue as to who was going to sit on the bright pink carpet square!

Alternatives to the carpet squares include using PE hoops, mathematical shapes which the children have to sit in front of, and numbered cards (the practitioner instructs children to sit by a number as they come into class).

Other strategies include:

♦ Ask the children to move if they are too close to someone before you begin teaching.
♦ Praise children for selecting a suitable space to sit/work in.
♦ When in a line ask the children to put their hand on the shoulder of the person in front of them and stand back so their arm is outstretched to create a good space between each other.
♦ Teach the children to use non-verbal gestures to stop children invading their personal space – a glare, an outstretched palm (Stop!).
♦ Ensure there is plenty of space around the classroom for children to work and move in.

'Stop! I don't like you doing that!' Very simple yet very effective – the outstretched hand is a brilliant way for children to get their message across to others without having to saying a word.

40. 'That's *woman's* work, that is!' Children who make sexist or racist comments

I have recently become aware of a child who has some rather alarming sexist and racist attitudes towards the female and ethnic minority pupils in my class. Even though this particular boy has not made these comments out loud, I have overheard him say them quietly to his friends. The things he has said have really upset me – what is the best way to tackle this behaviour?

Year 2 teacher

Children are usually very honest – if they like or dislike something or someone then they are not usually afraid to let others know about it, even though they may not be aware of how offensive or brutal their comments actually are. Their opinions may be based on their own thinking, yet most are influenced by any of the following:

◆ parents, siblings and other family members, particularly grandparents;
◆ carers/guardians;
◆ media – TV, radio, newspapers, magazines;
◆ internet;
◆ books;
◆ song lyrics;
◆ peers;
◆ other adults including practitioners.

Points to remember
◆ Everyone (children and adults) has different opinions on different topics of discussion.
◆ Everyone is entitled to their own opinions.
◆ Everyone should guard, wherever possible, from offending others with their views whether expressed in written or verbal form.

How do children in your class form, share and consider the impact of their views and ideas with others?

As highlighted in the quote at the start of this section, this behaviour has the potential to offend others and cause unnecessary unpleasantness in the classroom, resulting in potential fighting if children are angered by what they hear or read. So why do children make sexist and racist comments? Reasons include:

◆ learned behaviour – from influences identified previously;
◆ simply copying others;
◆ seeking a reaction from someone – attention seeking;
◆ used as an act of revenge;
◆ child thinks it is 'a big thing to say';
◆ low self-esteem – trying to put others down to make themselves feel better.

Clearly this behaviour is unacceptable in today's climate of political correctness and cultural sensitivity, and so practitioners need to act sooner rather than later to effectively manage it. As opposed to:

a) shouting at the child;
b) making them repeat what they have said in a loud voice to the rest of the class;
c) giving them a 40-minute lecture about how offensive their comments are, practitioners are encouraged to use any of the following:

◆ Remain calm in composure and tone of voice.
◆ Speak to the child on a one-to-one basis.
◆ Ask the child to explain why he thinks this way.
◆ Ask the child to consider the feelings of those she has passed comment on.
◆ Ask the child to consider how he would feel if he heard others making comments about his race/gender.
◆ Use PSHCE and circle time opportunities to challenge and discuss thinking relating to race and gender roles.
◆ State that you value her opinion yet make her aware of how offensive her comments are.
◆ Give the child some time out to think about what he has said and the impact it has had on others.
◆ Encourage the child to apologize to those she has offended, if appropriate.

Race and gender roles are potentially very sensitive topics for discussion and it is important for children to understand why this is the case and how certain viewpoints can be very damaging and harmful. Practitioners need to challenge children's thinking, offering different opinions and ideas so that they are able to consider the range of arguments presented and then make a personal decision with regard to where they stand in their own thinking.

Suggestions Box

Here are some ideas to help children to formulate more educated, non-biased, informed opinions relating to race and gender roles:

◆ Provide books and resources which promote diversity and images of women and men working in different roles.
◆ Invite people from the local community to talk to and work with the children – male nurse, female firefighter, a member of the Sikh community.
◆ Model appropriate language and terminology relating to gender roles and race.
◆ Devise activities which encourage diverse groupings – boys and girls, mixed race – with different children adopting certain roles and responsibilities.
◆ Establish links with schools with children from diverse backgrounds – organize collaborative projects and visits to promote cross-curricular learning and teaching, community spirit and celebrate diversity.

6 | Behaviours and children's personalities

41. '*I* know! I *knew* that! I know *everything*!' The Know-It-All in class

I work with a group of middle ability children and although I do not claim to know everything I do know what I have to teach. There is one child, however, who always seems to be trying to 'out do' me, claiming he knows more about a subject or topic than I do. Everything I say he states that he 'knew that!' I am getting really fed up of hearing it; the thing is if he did know then it would be all right but he doesn't! Help me please!

Year 6 student teacher

Every practitioner in every class will have at least one child (boy or girl) who claims to be an encyclopaedia of knowledge in human form. They have a tendency to interrupt others, 'lording' their accurate or inaccurate knowledge over the rest of the class which not only becomes an irritation for practitioners but also the child's peers.

While some children do actually have a wealth of accurate knowledge and understanding to share, many Know-It-All children really do not have this knowledge. We should therefore ask ourselves why they are doing this.

Key Questions

◆ Why do children pretend to be Know-It-Alls?
◆ How often do they pretend to know-it-all?
◆ Do Know-It-All children only pretend to know-it-all at school or does it interfere with other aspects of their life, e.g. at home? During a swimming lesson?

Talk to a colleague about your answers to these questions – does your thinking mirror or contradict theirs?

Children who pretend to be Know-It-Alls do it because of the following:

◆ attention seeking;
◆ low self-esteem;
◆ few friends;
◆ insecure with own knowledge;
◆ seeking a reaction;
◆ 'one-upmanship' syndrome – always trying to out do others;
◆ nervous habit.

Children who claim to know-it-all will do it at any time during the school day, particularly during the main teaching time in a lesson. This can become increasingly frustrating for practitioners who are trying to sustain a pace to their taught delivery as Know-It-Alls have a tendency to:

◆ shout out answers;
◆ interrupt peers and practitioners speaking;
◆ say 'I knew that' or 'I know that';
◆ take up valuable learning and teaching time by talking unnecessarily;
◆ deliberately sigh or look bored;
◆ laugh at others for incorrect answers.

To manage this behaviour practitioners are recommended to use the following strategies:

◆ Remain calm.
◆ Remind the child of the school/class rule relating to not interrupting others.
◆ Ask the child to explain herself on a one-to-one basis during the main activity time.
◆ Use parts of the child's answer, turning it into a correct one.
◆ Politely stop the child if he is taking up too much time explaining or answering something.
◆ Talk to the child about the dangers of becoming a Know-It-All in class – feelings of irritation and animosity from peers.
◆ Identify topics of interest and knowledge in all children – plan for activities which will allow all children to be 'Positive Know-It-Alls'.

Children who really are Know-It-Alls are prone to have very few friends and being bullied by their peers as their knowledge can be threatening and intimidating for others to appreciate, especially if the child continuously tries (and succeeds) in outdoing others. To support these children practitioners should:

◆ Ensure the children are on the Gifted and Talented register in school (if appropriate) – a separate IEP should be formulated.
◆ Design key questions specifically for them to answer during main teaching. Direct other questions to different groups – 'This question is for Gromit group to answer only . . .'
◆ Ensure work planned for the children is suitably challenging and differentiated so they do not become an issue while you are working with others.
◆ Invite the children to talk to the rest of the class about a certain topic or area of interest. Use a sand timer to ensure they do not overrun.
◆ Plan for these children to work with others of roughly the same intellect – putting them with lower ability children will cause issues.
◆ Allow them to access learning and teaching in other classes to challenge and develop current levels of attainment.

42. YAAAAWWWWWWN! The 'bored' child

In my 12 years of teaching I have never heard a child say they were bored in my class but a girl said it last week and I was devastated! She now keeps saying it even though I have tried everything I can to ensure that what she does in class is meaningful and stimulating. What am I to do?

Year 4 teacher

The phrase 'I'm bored!' is recognized by many in the teaching profession as the *worst* thing for a practitioner to hear being said by any of the children they teach. These two little words have the potential to destroy your confidence and self-esteem, particularly if said directly to you.

Top tips for initial management

◆ Try not to take the comment to heart (although it is very hard not to).

◆ Ensure you do not allow the child to see you are upset by his comments – crying in front of him is not a good idea!

◆ Remain calm and collected.

◆ Strategically ignore it – it might not be said again!

◆ Deal with your own emotions afterwards.

◆ Please do not take your anger and frustration out on the child – remember that you are a professional.

Children who say they are bored are usually seeking some sort of attention. Saying this to an adult usually results in the child either being guided towards an activity or being supported to refocus her attention on what she is doing. This is a strategy used by children who are simply lazy as the support offered is actually used to help them complete their work. However, there are a number of other reasons which underpin why a child may say he is bored:

◆ Child really is bored – lack of stimulation with the activities (all worksheet based learning) or the work is pitched at too low / too high a level for her (issues with differentiation and catering for Gifted and Talented).

◆ Child is tired – issues with sleeping patterns, home life, illness.

◆ Child is overstimulated by the creative and interactive activities planned for him – any activity which involves quietly reading or writing may not generate the same reaction from him as going pond dipping!

◆ Child has a habit of saying it yet she does not really mean it.

◆ Child may just need a change of environment – poor weather usually results in children staying inside their classrooms all day.

Reflection time

Consider the last time you personally were bored. Think about the context in which this happened, who you were with and at what time this boredom was generated. What did you do to 'revitalize' yourself? Make a note of your responses to these questions below:

_____

_____

_____

_____

_____

Are there times like this when the children you work with might experience this type of boredom? What could you do to ensure this does not occur?

Managing this behaviour can be very difficult especially if you are upset by the comment made. However, there are a number of recommended strategies you can adopt and implement to support your practice:

◆ Reflect on the activities you have provided for the child. Do they promote active learning?
◆ Ask the child calmly why he is feeling like this.
◆ Speak to the child about what she would like to do. Try to accommodate it in future lessons if/where appropriate.
◆ Integrate children's outside interests into the main teaching and independent activities to stimulate the learner.
◆ Talk to the children as a group in circle time about the notion of boredom and ways we can prevent this from becoming an issue.
◆ Plan for short periods of free choice activities throughout the day/week to sustain interest and engagement.

Practitioners can ensure that boredom never becomes an issue in their classroom if they use these preventative strategies:

◆ Plan for children to work in different groups – whole class, paired, friendship, gender.
◆ Integrate an element of challenge and competition into tasks and activities.
◆ Use ICT, film, music, dance, drama and PE to stimulate and sustain interest in lessons.
◆ Relate learning to a real-life context so children 'see the point'.
◆ Use drawings, painting, collages, models and photographs as a way to record learning.
◆ Take learning outside into the wider environment – trips, visits, walks.
◆ Avoid 'death by worksheet' – plan for practical activities.
◆ Plan for teaching to be delivered in short bursts, team teaching with your children.
◆ Rearrange the furniture in the classroom – rows of desks for 'Victorian School' day.

43. 'You'll *never* guess what . . . !' Children and idle gossiping

I have a good class but there are two girls who are real gossipers! They are always whispering to each other or are huddled in deep conversation. I am worried about this as none of the other children want to be friends with them due to some of the untrue things the girls have said about them. What can I do about these little 'gas bags'?!

Year 3 class teacher

Gossip is at best a waste of time, and at worst destructive. Girls are particularly prone to become gossipers from an early age as their linguistic capabilities are more developed than boys' and such behaviour is quite normal in female teenagers. This is not, however, to say that boys are adverse to a bit of 'back biting'.

Find Out!
◆ Are there more girl gossipers in your class in comparison to boys?
◆ How does this compare with classes further up/lower down in the school?
◆ Why do you think this is the case?

Many children get into the habit of gossiping through a range of influences which include:

◆ Practitioners 'chatting' in staffroom.
◆ TV – soap operas, chat shows.
◆ Music – derogatory lyrics.
◆ Radio – gossiping presenters.
◆ Magazines – gossip columns.
◆ Parents – gossiping with friends.

Top Tip!
We need to be mindful of these influences, ensuring that children are encouraged to pay more attention to their own life than those of others.

It is important to remember that not all gossip is bad and most of us like to indulge in a little idle gossip every now and then. This is completely normal and part of growing up. However, when children become so consumed by gossiping that it alters their opinion of others or their behaviour towards others, practitioners need to step in and ensure this does not become a real issue in the classroom.

Suggestions Box
◆ Ask the children to reflect on the feelings of those being talked about and those doing the gossiping – who do they have more empathy for? Why?
◆ Get the children to 'thought shower' the dangers and potential outcomes of idly gossiping about their best friend. Display these.
◆ Tell stories about children involved with idle gossiping.
◆ Use circle time and drama techniques to explore thoughts and feelings about gossiping.

Why is it that children engage in idle gossip? Possible reasons include:

- ◆ bored with activities in school;
- ◆ envy of others' belongings;
- ◆ jealousy of others' successes and achievements;
- ◆ resentment of others' abilities and skills;
- ◆ poor self-esteem – by speaking badly about others we try to convince ourselves we are fine the way we are.

In today's increasingly competitive world gossiping is one way for children to make them feel good about themselves. Work to build their self-esteem through written comments, smiles, verbal praise and displaying work so they feel they *can* be successful and achieve.

Scenario

A Year 4 class are undertaking gymnastics on the apparatus when Suzie suddenly bursts into tears and runs out of the hall. Fiona is sent to fetch the headteacher who finds Suzie sobbing in her classroom. After calming her down the headteacher discovers that two other girls in the class (Clare and Sharon) have been gossiping about Suzie, saying that she wears boys' underwear because her panties are dark blue.

If you were the headteacher what would you do?

a) Ignore Suzie and tell her to stop being silly?
b) Remove Clare and Sharon from the lesson and confront them with Suzie's accusations?
c) Speak to Clare and Sharon on an individual basis after the lesson? or
d) Talk to the class about the dangers of idle gossiping?

Discuss your decisions with your colleagues and then compare your thinking with the details provided below.

Selecting strategies c) and d) are better options as a) will make Suzie feel even worse and b) will provide the perfect opportunity for Clare and Sharon to jointly deny it!

All children should be made aware of how idle gossip is an unhealthy attitude towards life as it can make people bitter, unhappy and destroy relationships with others. To manage idle gossiping practitioners should:

◆ make it clear that idle gossiping will not be tolerated;
◆ make gossipers apologize for anything bad they have said about others;
◆ inform parents/carers about incidents involving idle gossip;
◆ ensure activities in school are engaging – children are less likely

to gossip about others if they are absorbed in what they are doing;

◆ have a class/school motto, e.g. 'If you can't say something nice about someone, then say nothing at all';

◆ promote peer positivity!

44. All on my own: The loner child

Whenever I am on playground duty I always notice one particular child who is sat on her own, not playing or talking to anyone. She does not make any effort to play with the other children and even when I try to get her involved in others' games she plays for two minutes and then goes back to sitting on her own. What can I do about this?

Key Stage 1 Higher Level Teaching Assistant

While most children are bright, sociable and outgoing there are some who are quiet, reserved and quite solitary by their own nature. Some simply like to be on their own and there are times when all children should be encouraged to have some time alone so they can appreciate the value of these moments for private reflection or a chance to build up energy levels.

There is nothing wrong with children who seem perfectly content to be on their own. Practitioners may, however, wish to encourage these children to become more actively involved with other children as and when appropriate so they practically appreciate the benefits of friendship, collaboration and team spirit.

Questions to answer

◆ Are there many children who are loners in your class/school?

◆ How do you personally feel about their behaviour? Does it upset you or are you not concerned by it?

◆ Do you try to do anything about this behaviour during the school day? If so, what do you try to do? Is it successful? If not, why do you not interfere with their behaviour?

Children who prefer to be alone usually concern practitioners as they are so used to seeing children working and playing harmoniously together (most of the time!) on a daily basis. While it is good practice to support and encourage loners to become more involved with others in the class/school, this can actually do more harm than good as the child may feel pressured to conform with perceived expectations of what children should be like, as opposed to them feeling comfortable being in their own company.

Activity
Children who are loners demonstrate certain behaviours. Use a pen and 'put a line through' the behaviours and attributes noted below which do not apply to children who prefer to be on their own:

Sits alone and away from others
Quiet workers
Likes working with others sometimes
Loud and abrasive
Outgoing and lively
Softly spoken
Happy to help others
Self-absorbed
Shy and apprehensive
Calm and collected
Few or no friends
Happy and smiley
Good listener
Always involved with others
Willing to try something new
Low in confidence and self-esteem

Interestingly some loners are actually happy and smiley although this is more of an internal personal feeling as opposed to a disposition clearly shown by their body language or the way they speak and interact with others – loners are just simply better in their own company than with others. Loners should not be confused with children who are friendless – some are just a victim of their own immature, brusque, aggressive or extrovert nature. These children find that others in their class cannot relate to them and so are found sat 'alone on the bench'. If this is the case practitioners should work to develop the social skills of these children.

Reasoning behind why children are loners is quite varied as shown below:

◆ Low confidence levels.
◆ Poor speech and/or social skills.
◆ Differing interests from those of their peers.
◆ Peers are not of the same intellectual level/maturity.
◆ Personality trait born with – prefers own company.
◆ Poor self-esteem.

So is it necessary to manage their behaviour? Well, this is all dependent on whether their behaviour hinders their ability to make progress academically and socially. Some recommendations are presented for practitioners to evaluate and adopt as their own practice below:

Do	Don't
◆ Make them feel part of the class – acknowledge their presence wherever possible, ask them specific questions to draw them into the work of the class. ◆ Plan for very small group work (2–3 children). ◆ Ensure the children they work with are not dominating, yet are patient and caring. ◆ Talk to the class about everyone being different – celebrate these by having a 'Jack Day' or a 'Claire Day'. ◆ Use them as a model for 'good working' or 'calm behaviour'.	◆ Make children feel guilty for being a loner. ◆ Force them to do anything they are not comfortable doing. ◆ Put them in large group activities. ◆ Pair them up with loud or extrovert children.

45. 'Look at me! Look at me! La la la!' The class 'clown'

I like sharing a joke and having a laugh with my class, and I encourage the children in my class to do the same. There is, however, one child who likes to be the class clown and deliberately drops things, acts silly and generally makes a bit of a fool of himself. I dread to think what will happen to him when he goes up to secondary school. How can I help him and manage his behaviour?

Year 6 teacher

Most classes will have a class clown – a child who likes to be the centre of comical attention – and will do this by any means possible.

> **How do they do it?**
> How do class clowns seek attention in your class? Make a list of as many ways as you can think of them achieving 'clown status' within three minutes. Your time begins . . . NOW!
>
> ◆ _____
> ◆ _____
> ◆ _____
> ◆ _____
> ◆ _____
> ◆ _____
> ◆ _____
> ◆ _____
> ◆ _____

As the activity above highlights, class clowns will do anything to establish their 'role' among their peers. Interestingly, you do not need to have 20 years' teaching experience or much knowledge of a particular class to be able to spot the clown:

Fact file: Class Clown

SEX: Usually male.
AGE: Anything between 3 and 11 years.
ACADEMIC ABILITY: Limited yet could achieve if he applied himself to work.
SOCIAL SKILLS: Developing.
REASONS FOR BEHAVIOUR: Various – considers it 'cool' to be the 'entertainer' of the class, hiding academic or social inadequacies, thinks it is the way to get peers to like him, does not know when to stop playing the fool, bored, immature.
REGARDED BY PEERS: A fool yet sometimes 'funny'.
PRACTITIONER'S THOUGHTS: Have potential to be real nuisance and cause great disruption to teaching and the children's learning.

Class clowns relish the reaction they get from their peers and practitioners, whether it be in the form of laughter, a stern 'look' or verbal disapproval. It is important that practitioners do not show that the child's behaviour is getting to them – if you do the children know they have 'got you' and know how far they can push the boundaries of behaviour with you.

Activity

Effectively managing the behaviour of class clowns will only occur if the practitioner selects the most appropriate strategies for their children. With this in mind consider your specific class clown and grade each of the strategies below using the following key:

A = Excellent strategy
B = Good strategy
C = Fair strategy
D = Poor strategy

Implement strategies only you consider to be A or B standard.

Ignore her. **Grade:**	Laugh along with her. **Grade:**	Sit child on his own. **Grade:**
Send him out of class for a few moments. **Grade:**	Move her to another space in the classroom. **Grade:**	Keep the child in at play/dinnertime. **Grade:**
Send child to Foundation One or Two 'as she is behaving like a Foundation child'. **Grade:**	Remain calm and ask the child to stop being silly. **Grade:**	Give the child a choice – stop behaviour or do some extra homework. **Grade:**
Use your 'practitioner glare'. **Grade:**	Consult parents/carers about your concerns. **Grade:**	Talk to the child on a one-to-one about her behaviour. **Grade:**
Catch him being good. **Grade:**	Ask peers to comment on their views of the 'clown'. **Grade:**	Send child to the headteacher. **Grade:**
Acknowledge and praise those who are being 'mature'. **Grade:**	Raise your voice at her. **Grade:**	Distract the child with a request, question or task. **Grade:**
Use a warning system specific for the child. **Grade:**	Up the pace of delivery and teaching. **Grade:**	Respond to him with sarcastic jibes. **Grade:**

To prevent class clowns from turning your classroom into a circus, a number of simple preventative measures can be put in place. These include:

◆ Set high expectations of behaviour right from the beginning of the year.
◆ Praise, reward and acknowledge behaviours you like to see in your class.
◆ Plan stimulating activities which respond and engage the children via their different learning styles.
◆ Use the school's behaviour policy to ensure silly behaviours are dealt with using structures and approaches used throughout the school.

46. '*I* didn't do it!' Children who tell lies

If there is one thing I cannot stand it is a child lying. It makes me really angry to know certain children blatantly lie and I find it hard professionally to have a positive relationship with these children because I cannot trust them. I saw a girl this morning playing on her mobile phone and when I asked her to put it away she said she did not have a phone! I really would like to know how I can manage this behaviour.

Year 6 teaching assistant

Most adults regard lying as a major disciplinary issue which can develop into something more serious if it is not managed quickly and effectively. It is important to remember that we all lie, whether it is a little white fib, a 'story' to smooth tricky situations over, or a full-blown barefaced 'whopper'. Lies are used to attempt false denial, false blame, false excuses and apparent ignorance.

Children from the age of three tell lies because they have a good idea that lying may prevent them getting into trouble for something they have said or done. Another key reason relates to trying to impress others, which boys are more prone to using in an attempt to try to win the hand of their first girlfriend through boasting and male bravado! Girls, on the other hand lie to win friendships and stay 'in the group'.

While it is sometimes difficult to recognize 'fact from fiction' there are ways in which we can tell if a child is telling a lie.

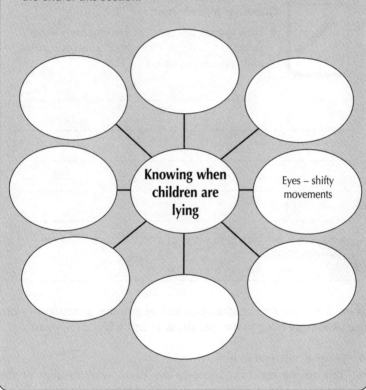

Activity
Using the diagram below fill in the blank spaces by identifying ways in which you can tell when a child may be lying. Once you have completed this task compare your answers to those offered at the end of this section.

Knowing when children are lying

Eyes – shifty movements

It is most probably not the little white lies which children tell that upset practitioners; it is more the big lies which the practitioner clearly knows are not true. Lies might include:

◆ Saying they have left their homework in their bedroom when you know they have a history of not doing any at all!
◆ Talking to their friend when you asked for silence and you watched them defy you!

◆ Telling their friends that they get £20 a week pocket money when you know the child has recently been put onto free school meals.
◆ Writing in their weekend journal that they won their 200 metre swimming badge even though you still work with the child who is in the non-swimmers' group when the class goes to the pool.

Questions for reflection
◆ How would you react to the situations above? Select any one of them and note your ideas and approaches below:

_____

_____

_____

_____

_____

Compare your notes to the strategies for effective management presented below.

There are a number of strategies and approaches practitioners can use to manage lying in the classroom as and when it happens:

◆ Strategically ignore it.
◆ Talk to the child on a one-to-one basis, warning him of the dangers and potential consequences of lying.
◆ Give the children the opportunity to tell you the truth when they are ready to.
◆ Inform the headteacher/parents about your concerns regarding frequent liars.
◆ Tell the children that you know they must feel worried about you being cross but that you are not angry and that you understand.
◆ Tell them that you do not like children lying and that you would rather they be honest with you.

To prevent lying becoming an issue in your class there are a number of preventative measures practitioners can adopt:

◆ Use circle time to talk about why people lie and the issues surrounding doing it.
◆ Establish honest relationships with the class by praising children who are honest in difficult situations.
◆ Use PHSCE teaching time to talk about the importance of being truthful in society.
◆ Read *The Boy Who Cried Wolf* to the children during an assembly/collective worship. Discuss the reasoning behind the unfortunate yet avoidable consequences of the tale.

Answers to Activity

Possible ways to tell if a child is lying include:

◆ Eyes – shifty eye movements particularly to the left, gazing intensely at you, and rapid rate of blinking.
◆ Body – fidgety or awkward hand movements, stroking their hair, rubbing hands together, restless feet or leg movements.
◆ Nose – touching this frequently.
◆ Mouth – covering this with a hand, finger touching the side of the mouth, false looking smiles.
◆ Face – keeping a very 'straight face'.
◆ Speech – providing longwinded explanations, providing little detail, slower delivery, increased number of pauses between words and sentences, slightly higher pitch of voice.
◆ Saying one thing to one person and changing the story when recounting it to another.

---

47. 'Umm . . . well . . . erm . . . well . . . I . . . '
Shyness in the classroom

As it is their final year in primary school I work hard to ensure the children have a bit of character and confidence about them before they move up to secondary school. There is one boy (Jack) though who is painfully shy and it has a real effect on virtually every aspect of his school life – from working with other children to dinnertime to answering questions. How can I help him to overcome his shyness?

Year 6 teacher

Everyone has at one time or another in their life been shy. Social anxiety, as it is referred to, is a very common condition for people to have to manage – nine out of ten of us confess to suffering from it at some stage in our lives.

Questions for reflection

◆ When was the last time you suffered from shyness/anxiety?
◆ In what context or situation was it?
◆ Why did you become shy? How did it make you feel?
◆ What did you do about it?

Consider your responses to these questions with regard to shy children you know in your class – are they very similar or different?

Many people put shyness down to genes as some say that shy parents will rear shy children. Indeed, shy people do produce more stress hormones than others but this is not to say that genetics is the only reason and that shyness cannot be overcome. Shyness is directly linked to levels of confidence and anxiety, and is usually exhibited as a result of one of two main contexts explored below:

Context	Description	Consequences of behaviour
Social situations	Children become shy when they meet new people or work in different settings.	Fewer friends, less intimacy (as an adult) and potential depression and loneliness.
Timidity and fear of change	Child finds it difficult to cope with new routines and ways of working.	Apprehension, nervousness and higher anxiety levels.

Shyness can also be the result of the following:

◆ a previous deeply traumatic experience;
◆ being bullied;
◆ a natural disposition;
◆ overpowering parents/carers or practitioners;
◆ attention seeking;
◆ low self-esteem;
◆ poor social skills;
◆ limited communication skills.

Shyness can be a crippling experience as it can really hold children back. From talking to others to making friends to getting changed in front of others for PE – shyness can prevent children from being involved in activities they want and need to be involved in.

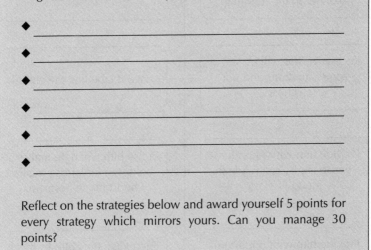

What would you do?

Consider the child described by the Year 6 teacher at the start of this section. What strategies would you put in place to support this child and help him to overcome his shyness? Talk with a colleague and make a note of your ideas below:

◆ _____

◆ _____

◆ _____

◆ _____

◆ _____

◆ _____

Reflect on the strategies below and award yourself 5 points for every strategy which mirrors yours. Can you manage 30 points?

There are a number of ways in which shyness can be conquered. These include:

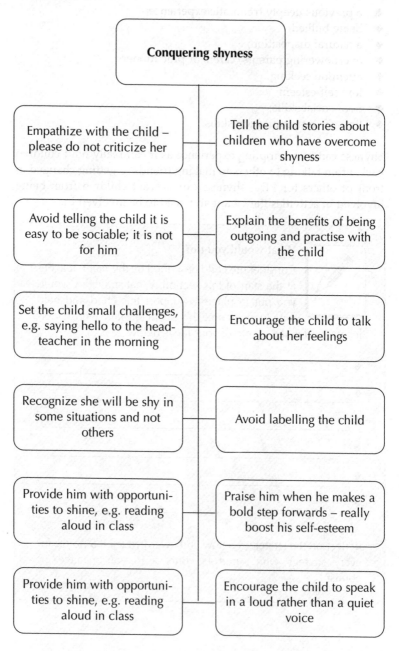

Conquering shyness

Empathize with the child – please do not criticize her

Tell the child stories about children who have overcome shyness

Avoid telling the child it is easy to be sociable; it is not for him

Explain the benefits of being outgoing and practise with the child

Set the child small challenges, e.g. saying hello to the head-teacher in the morning

Encourage the child to talk about her feelings

Recognize she will be shy in some situations and not others

Avoid labelling the child

Provide him with opportunities to shine, e.g. reading aloud in class

Praise him when he makes a bold step forwards – really boost his self-esteem

Provide him with opportunities to shine, e.g. reading aloud in class

Encourage the child to speak in a loud rather than a quiet voice

It is important to remember that being shy does not condemn children or adults to an unhappy life. In fact, given time and a little support children can easily lose their feelings of social awkwardness and go on to have academic, professional and personal success. Even if children do grow up to be shy adults, they will usually prove themselves to be empathetic and respond sensitively to others.

A year later . . .

While undertaking some transition work between Year 6 and 7 with the local secondary school, the Year 6 teacher (who introduced this behaviour to us) was walking down a school corridor when she was stopped by a male Year 7 pupil.

'Hello, Miss!' said the young man, a wide smile on his face. 'Do you remember me?'

The Year 6 teacher looked carefully and it suddenly dawned on her as to who it was.

'Jack?! Is that you?' she asked, amazed.

'Yeah! How are you, Miss?'

The conversation which followed highlighted how Jack had 'come out of his shell' in secondary school and was now 'flying high' on the academic front. He was top in all of his classes, was a valuable member of the school football team and had just made friends with a 'certain young lady'.

Being shy may be just a passing phase. Do remember that when *you* are shy the next time . . . it will pass!

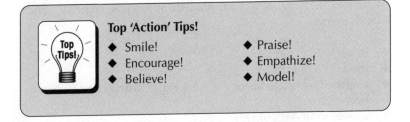

Top 'Action' Tips!

- ◆ Smile!
- ◆ Encourage!
- ◆ Believe!

- ◆ Praise!
- ◆ Empathize!
- ◆ Model!

48. Tears flowing freely! Children who cry in class

There are two children in my class who are what I would call real cry babies!
Tears spring from their eyes for every reason thinkable and it is having an
effect on their ability to remain focused and engage with their schoolwork.
How can I help them to prevent all of their paper-based work becoming
crinkly when it dries out?

Year 1 teacher

While the practitioner above is rather flippant about this behaviour,
it is important to remember that labelling children who cry in class
as 'cry babies' is not recommended. Children who cry need to be
supported and it is vital practitioners work with parents/carers and
the children themselves to ensure their emotions do not interfere
with their education.

What do you think?
Reflect on the practitioner's comments above.
What do you think about the practitioner's
'description' of the children? What reasons can
you think of as to why these children might cry
during the day? What strategies would you use to manage any
two of the reasons you have identified?

Seeing and hearing children cry is an unsettling experience for any
practitioner as it usually shows children at their most emotional and
vulnerable. Most practitioners immediately attempt to seek out the
reason as to why the child is crying, yet many children are so upset
that it is difficult for them to articulate themselves or catch their
breath properly.

Children may cry for a great number of reasons, some of which
include being:

- in pain;
- tired;
- confused – unclear about the work set or instructions given;
- hot/cold;
- unable to sit with or work with friends;
- attention seeking;

- part of their personality – a tearful disposition;
- hungry;
- bullied – hurt by other children's comments;
- lonely;
- distressed – issues at home including illness, death or abuse in the family;
- scared – of peers, practitioners, parents/carers, the work set;
- thirsty.

Top Tips!

- Avoid getting the child to explain why she is upset straightaway. Let her calm down first.
- Have a box of tissues to hand to mop any tears and wipe any noses!
- Give children a 'comfort teddy' to hug.
- Offer soothing words which empathize with the child's feelings.
- Use other practitioners or parent helpers if an incident occurs during main teaching time.

Essential Action

If a child regularly comes to school crying and you suspect they are being abused or neglected in any way, you must inform the practitioner who has Child Protection responsibilities immediately who will report it if they think it is appropriate. However, if nothing is done it is every teacher's right to report matters to Social Services.

Children who cry have the potential to disrupt others in the class as the sound or sight of their peers sobbing will usually elicit real concern in them – it is not uncommon for children to focus their attention solely on the 'crier', stroking his back and offering words of empathy while you attempt to teach the class how to add three numbers together!

Case Study

A girl in a Year 1 class would cry as her class filed into school in the morning due to the fact that she began to miss her mum. Inconsolable, the girl would not calm down until the start of the second lesson of the day. As this was having a negative effect on the girl's learning, the lead practitioner discussed the issue with the parents and together they devised a simple strategy by which the girl would come into class with her mum before the bell sounded and undertake some simple tasks set by the practitioner for the girl to do. As the girl became engrossed in the activities her mum would quietly leave . . .

In most situations offering a little support to the child is sufficient to calm her. The art of distraction – engaging the child in a stimulating activity (ICT, for example) or making a little joke – is a useful approach to adopt as well. To manage tears relating to the work set practitioners should ensure:

◆ the subject matter is taught in a lively and uncomplicated manner;
◆ the work is differentiated appropriately;
◆ the work is appropriate to the child's learning needs;
◆ the work is explained clearly;
◆ the children can complete it in the time given;
◆ strategies for support are available, e.g. use of other adults, dictionaries.

For tears shed due to issues with friendships practitioners can:

◆ use circle time opportunities to settle arguments and incidents anonymously;
◆ provide time for children to talk through incidents outside main teaching time – playtime, dinnertime;
◆ organize games for children to play in friendship teams on the playground to rebuild relationships.

7 | Behaviours and social skills

49. 'Where are your manners?' The children with no manners

Why is it children in our classrooms today just do not seem to have any manners? The phrases 'Please', 'Thank you' and 'Excuse me' seem completely alien to some of them! How can I make my children more 'mannered'?

Year 3 teacher

Many practitioners would agree that manners 'cost nothing'. Most adults use their manners out of respect and politeness so our lives with others remain civilized and on good terms. We have learned the importance of using manners appropriately with years of experience, yet many children today appear rude, obnoxious and completely oblivious to the fact that being well-mannered is just plain common courtesy.

Manners in action!

During either a morning or afternoon session make a note of the number of times children use their manners appropriately without being reminded to. Compare it with another practitioner's class. How well do your children compare?

There are a number of reasons as to why children do not use their manners appropriately. These include:

◆ Parental/carer influences do not encourage children to use their manners.
◆ Role models (TV, music) do not appear to actively use their manners.

◆ Current children's 'attitudes' do not seem to favour the use of manners.

◆ Practitioners are so focused on delivering the curriculum that they forget the importance of developing and sustaining the social skills of the children they work with.

Children very regularly forget to use their manners. They must be taught to use them at every given opportunity so it becomes second nature for them to use 'Please' and 'Thank you' without having to be reminded by an adult.

When and where?

Make a list of all the possible opportunities children can use and apply their manners throughout a school day. Consider key times during the day when manners are very important for the children to use. Observe children during these times and note if they use their manners or not.

There are a number of ways in which manners can be actively promoted in the classroom:

◆ Praise children who use their manners without being prompted.

◆ Use circle time and PSHCE opportunities to discuss the importance of manners in all aspects of life.

◆ Create 'Manner Monitors' who 'listen out' for manners being used during the day.

◆ Create a 'Marvellous Manners' display chart which is frequently used to monitor levels of manners and who is marvellously mannered!

◆ Use drama to explore the thoughts and feelings of characters that do/do not use their manners.

◆ Have a well-mannered badge for the day which is given to one child who is well-mannered to all with whom they come into contact.

◆ Ask the children to remind you of what you like to hear when you take the dinner register – 'Dinners, *please!*'

◆ Use the classic phrase, 'What's the magic word?'

Case Study

A practitioner working with Year 6 was so appalled by the poor manners of the children that she devised a simple yet effective management strategy to encourage the children to use their manners more frequently. She would take a tambourine into class with her and whenever she heard a child forget their manners she would shake the tambourine. The group of children she was working with had been trained to collectively say, 'Where are your manners?' to the 'manner-less' child. By using peer pressure the practitioner was able to encourage the use of manners in the classroom without having to open her mouth!

There will always be individuals who forget to use their manners. Sometimes this is accidental, other times it is because the child does not care for using them. Again, there are a number of strategies to manage this behaviour:

◆ Use the 'practitioner glare' to remind the child of her 'missing manners'.

◆ If distributing some paper to individuals hold onto the paper until the child has said, 'Thank you' – only then should you release your grip.

◆ Ask class monitors who are handing out pens, rulers and crayons around the class to identify children who are saying 'Thank you'.

◆ Take back resources which children are using if they did not say 'Please' or 'Thank you' when they should have done. Do they know what they forgot to say?

Above all children should be made to understand the importance of being well-mannered in today's society. Oh yes, and if they do use their manners, *make sure they mean it!*

50. Push, pushes, pushing, pushed!
Children who push in/push others

My class have been trained to line up appropriately from the start of the year yet there is one child who always tries to push his way into the line. He does not care who he hurts in the process – he just sees where he wants to be and charges straight towards it. As he has a rather stocky build there have been some real incidents resulting from his actions. What can I do to ensure he stops hurting others?

Year 2 teacher

Children have to line up for a number of reasons – assembly, play-time, fire alarm – and at many different times during the school day. While most children are happy to stand anywhere in the line, there are certain children who either have to be first, last or next to their friends. If they are not quick enough these children find themselves 'out of place' and this usually results in children trying to push into the line, upsetting and disturbing others.

Find Out!
Observe your class when they line up during one day. Make a note (mental or written) of which children always want to be first in the line or who have a tendency to push in. Consider the reasons why these children behave in this way.

If ineffectively managed, this behaviour has the potential to delay children going out to play, having their dinner on time or leaving school with everyone else! Children who push in the line may stamp on other children's feet, barge sharply into other children's chests or physically knock them over. They may even pinch, kick or bite others. It has been known for pushers to knock a whole class to the ground like a set of dominoes due to the close proximity of the rest of the class.

Children who push in must be taught that it is unacceptable to do this. They need to be removed from the line and placed somewhere else which is safer and more sensible for them. They should also apologize to those children they may have hurt. Other recommended strategies include:

◆ Always ensure two minutes are set aside before the children have to go into assembly / the dinner hall to prevent issues occurring.

◆ Walk along the line and move children away from others whom you know will cause an issue as they move from the classroom.

◆ Organize the lines in different ways, e.g. girls first, black hair first, birthdays in summer at the back, table by table, all those who like fish as pets in the middle of the line, height order, age order (oldest first, i.e. the lead practitioner!).

◆ Create the lines by moving into them in different ways, e.g. a penguin, a mouse, a frog.

◆ Teach the children to stand with a little gap between them and the person in front/behind them, so that if someone does need to step into the line they can with out trampling on toes!

◆ Allow the children to organize the line – one child (A) stands and selects one person (B) to stand behind them, B stands and selects C who selects D etc.

◆ Praise good lining up.

Case Study

To prevent pushing and arguments relating to who was going to be first and last in the line, a Year 2 teacher created 'Line Monitors'. These were two different children selected at the start of each day. Each was given a badge to wear, one saying 'Front' and the other saying 'Back' indicating the positions they were to take up in the line every time the class had to line up. These monitors would then walk up and down the line, organizing the children to ensure it was straight and quiet. By giving some of the children an authoritative role, practitioners had less behavioural issues to deal with! That is until play time arrived . . . !

To prevent pushers disturbing the line and hurting others, practitioners are encouraged to use the following ideas and approaches:

◆ Talk to the pusher about how his behaviour is upsetting and hurting others.

◆ Use role play and drama activities to explore ways to deal with feelings of frustration and anger at not getting the space she would like in an imaginary line.

◆ Create line up rules with the class during PSHCE. Display these above the classroom door or suspend them from the ceiling so all children can see and be reminded of them.

◆ Create a class song about lining up or sing a song all the children like as they line up.

51. 'All you've got to give me is a little R.E.S.P.E.C.T.' Being respectful in the classroom

I have been in the teaching profession for over 20 years and I still love working with children. I do, however, dislike the increasing level of disrespect I seem to find in my classes. How can I instil more respect in the 'youth of today' who are in danger of becoming the 'rude adults of the future'?

Year 4 teacher

Defining the term
◆ What do we mean by the term 'respect'?
◆ How does it relate to child and adult life?
◆ What qualities or attributes do people have which make them 'respectful'?
◆ How are children being disrespectful?

Make a note of your ideas below:

_____

_____

_____

_____

_____

Compare your ideas with one or more of your colleagues – how does your thinking compare?

Many children (and adults for that matter) find it difficult to define the term 'respect' as dictionary explanations are either confusing or lacking in clarity. Most of us think of respect as the appropriate use of manners, looking after one's own or others' property, and ensuring others have certain levels of privacy. However, respect encompasses more than that as the diagram below shows:

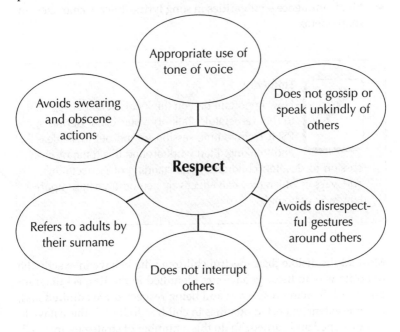

The whole notion of respect operates on different levels, these being respect for:

◆ the individual (himself/herself);
◆ each other (peers and siblings);
◆ their elders (parents and other adults);
◆ their environment (classroom, school, home, community).

It is said by some practitioners that the rising levels of violence and antisocial behaviour in our communities today is a result of a lack of respect, in not only children but adults too. So why do we find more and more children being disrespectful? Factors which have influenced this change include:

◆ Poor modelling of respectful behaviours in parents, carers and practitioners.
◆ Lack of expectations from adults.
◆ Increased use of bad and slang language in day-to-day conversations.
◆ Seen as excitingly 'rebellious' to answer adults back.
◆ Media influence – vulgarities in song lyrics, 'bitchy' characters in soap operas.

Find Out!

How important do you think children believe it is to be respectful? Talk to your class during a PSHCE/circle time session to find out their ideas and thinking. Plan work around this topic of discussion to develop children's understanding of respectfulness and ways in which they can effectively demonstrate this important 'way of being'.

Most adults dislike disrespectful children who behave in exactly the opposite way to those behaviours identified in the Respect diagram on page 165. Being respectful and being respected are admired and, to some extent, expected qualities in children today yet these have to be developed and earned. To do this a number of strategies are available for practitioners to select, modify and implement:

◆ Model respectful behaviours so the children see them 'in practice'.
◆ Praise those who are respectful of others.
◆ Listen to children with your whole attention.
◆ Use whole class reward systems to promote respectful behaviours, e.g. marbles in the jar.
◆ Make a list of respectful behaviours and display these. Review them regularly – 'Which behaviours are you going to show others today?'
◆ Use drama and role play to explore scenarios which involve or require different respectful behaviours.
◆ Ask the children to identify and bring in pictures of people whom they respect. List the qualities they have and encourage

the children to aspire to be like them by modelling their appropriate behaviours in school.

◆ Ask parents/carers to monitor how respectful their children are being outside school. Ensure the children are well-rewarded for their efforts.

◆ Read stories about characters that are respectful or disrespectful. Ask them to identify which character they like, discussing why they feel this way.

Fact: If your pupils respect you, and feel that you respect them, this will inevitably lead to better behaviour in your classroom.

If respect from others needs to be earned, then practitioners need to know how they can earn this from the children they teach. Ways this can be achieved include:

◆ Being a good role model.
◆ Avoiding shouting.
◆ Being firm but fair.
◆ Always remaining consistent in your approach to everything.
◆ Showing that you care.
◆ Empathizing; not criticizing.
◆ Supporting others without question or hesitation.
◆ Striking a balance between practitioner and human being.
◆ Remembering your 'Please's' and 'Thank you's'.
◆ Making people feel good about themselves.
◆ Smiling and sharing a joke.
◆ Listening to others.

Remember! The same applies to children who wish to be respected by their peers and elders.

52. 'RARRRRR!' Terrible temper tantrums

There is a five-year-old in my class who has terrible temper tantrums, particularly when he does not get his own way! I thought these only happened during the 'terrible twos'. What's the best way to manage these tantrums?
Year 1 teacher, NQT

Contrary to popular belief, the 'terrible twos' can actually become the 'terrible threes', 'fours' or even more until the child's communication skills, maturity and understanding develop sufficiently to allow her to control her own emotions. While the example above highlights the behaviour in a boy, it is not gender-specific. Children having a tantrum will usually involve them doing one or more of the following:

◆ screaming;
◆ crying;
◆ shouting;
◆ stamping their feet;
◆ punching the air;
◆ throwing things around the room;
◆ a combination of all the above at the same time!

While some children's tantrums can build up very gradually, in others they can be a sudden explosion of raw emotion. A tantrum can last from between ten seconds to over half-an-hour depending on the situation (the cause), the child's feelings and the way in which the behaviour is managed.

These factors affect the potential for a tantrum to disrupt a class. It would be impossible for children to not be distracted by the behaviours highlighted above. There is a tendency sometimes for children to watch and comment on what they are seeing, either becoming embarrassed or frightened of the child, or laughing at them.

Most tantrums develop as a result of wants, perceived needs and desires not being fulfilled with immediate effect. Without a positive outcome, tantrums are a way in which children can express their feelings of desperation, anger and frustration at a situation.

While having established the potential causes of the tantrum, it is important to recognize the 'warning signs' so you know when a tantrum is just about to take place. This then gives you time to prepare yourself! Warning signs include:

◆ being irritated by other children's behaviours;
◆ being overcompetitive when engaged in game play – child has to win at all costs;
◆ having aggressive body and spoken language;
◆ being easily upset by trivial events – tears are shed quickly;
◆ whining or complaining about others.

Identifying the causes

Using the diagram below fill in the blank spaces by identifying possible reasons why a child may have a tantrum. Once you have completed this task compare your answers to those offered at the end of this section.

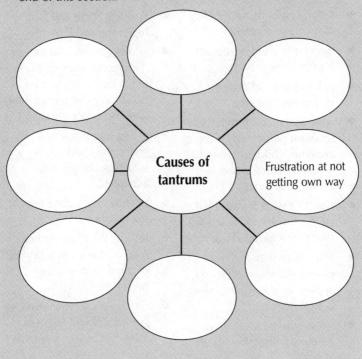

Causes of tantrums

Frustration at not getting own way

Strategies for effective/ineffective management are varied yet specific:

Do ensure you . . .	Do ensure you avoid . . .
◆ keep your cool; ◆ tell the child that her behaviour is unacceptable; ◆ ignore the child or distract him in some way; ◆ talk to the child near the end of her tantrum; ◆ remove the child from the situation particularly if there are other children around – he can become embarrassed or anxious; ◆ consider what is causing the tantrum; work to ensure this situation is avoided again; ◆ empathize with the child – ensure she knows that you appreciate the feelings she is experiencing; ◆ inform the parents/carers. Assess whether this occurs at home; ◆ offer the child alternative ways to manage his emotions – deep breathing, playing with blue tack, time out, talking to an adult.	◆ shouting back at the child; ◆ standing there and laughing at the child; ◆ allowing other children in the class to manage the behaviour – this can be potentially dangerous if the child becomes physical; ◆ giving into blackmail – giving the child sweets/stickers is not acceptable; ◆ bearing any grudge after the tantrum; ◆ leaving the child on her own as she is not in a state of mind to look after herself properly; ◆ totally ignore the behaviour – the child will begin to think this is an acceptable way to behave; ◆ frightening the child in any way – physically harming a child will result in you losing your job; ◆ backing down. Changing the situation to meet the child's wants means the child will expect this every time. Avoid this at all costs.

Answers to Identifying the causes

Possible causes include:
◆ Hunger – not enough or a lack of breakfast.
◆ Sadness – loss of family pet, just had an argument with friend.
◆ Frustration – unable to express him/herself verbally.
◆ Anger – feelings of unfairness, family difficulties.
◆ Tiredness or exhaustion – lack of quality sleep.
◆ Home influences – child is used to getting her own way.

53. 'Hey you – it's *my* turn!' Taking turns in the classroom

It might be just be me but it seems to be a constant battle in my class to get the children to take turns with . . . well . . . anything really! Toys, the computer, bikes outside – everything seems to cause an 'incident'. How can I teach the art of taking turns to children who don't want to take them (turns I mean!)?

Nursery practitioner

Taking turns is an important yet very difficult behaviour for young children particularly to develop, although it continues to be an issue for some children right through their primary years at school. It is an essential skill, not only in the sense of playing a game (board game), but also in many aspects of everyday life – queuing up for the bus, sharing information in a meeting, paying for items at the supermarket.

Reflection task

When does turn-taking become an issue for you in your classroom? Observe your class during one lesson, noting when there is an issue (time), who was involved (boys, girls, mixture, pairs, groups) and why it occurred. Use the chart overleaf to help you record your observations.

Time	Who	Why

Reasons as to why children find it difficult to take turns are varied as you may have found from undertaking the task above. These include:

◆ the child is an only child and does not have to take turns with anything at home;
◆ parents/practitioners have not taught child to take turns with peers;
◆ impulsiveness;
◆ immaturity;
◆ lack of patience;
◆ frustration;
◆ not enough toys to play with/resources to use;
◆ 'me me me' syndrome – child is self-centred and believes he can have what he wants when he wants;
◆ lack of understanding.

With the potential to disrupt others, it is important to have to a number of ways in which practitioners can manage this behaviour.

If young children do not have enough toys to play with then the inevitable will happen – they will fight over them. Work to teach children how to share and take turns with resources. Let's hope Funky Monkey doesn't lose an arm!

Activity

Sort the strategies out below into effective and ineffective approaches to managing turn-taking issues. Write on the line by the side of the strategy either an E for effective or I for ineffective based on your own professional thinking.

◆ Be consistent in the rules of turn-taking. _____
◆ Model appropriate language linked to turn-taking, e.g. 'It is your turn now. It is mine after your go.' _____
◆ Teach the child to snatch the toy/object back if they had it first. _____
◆ Praise the children for waiting their turn. _____
◆ Let children sort out their turn-taking issues themselves. _____
◆ Play simple games, e.g. Lotto, Snap and Connect Four so that children practically appreciate the need for turn-taking. _____
◆ Have a 'turn taker' of the day – a person who is a perfect model of turn-taking in class. _____

Case Study

A Reception practitioner was becoming increasingly frustrated by the arguments which took place when the children accessed the outdoor play equipment, particularly with regard to the new tricycles the setting had purchased. One evening the practitioner was boiling eggs at home when she came up with an interesting way to ensure every child could take a turn with the equipment in as fair a way as possible. She brought in some egg timers which were shown to the children. The practitioner explained that the children could only go on the tricycles if they had a timer and when all of the sand had fallen through it. This then needed to be shown to the child on the tricycle so that they knew it was someone else's turn. It turned out to be a very visual and effective way to manage this behaviour!

Practitioners should also be mindful of ways that issues relating to turn-taking can be prevented in the classroom:

◆ Display charts by the side of activities – children need to put a smiley face by their name to indicate they have had a go.
◆ Use tags – buttons on a ribbon, sticky labels – to indicate whose turn it is to play, for example, in the home corner area.
◆ Create a class set of rules with the children. Talk with them about the importance of turn-taking in class.
◆ Use circle time and PSHCE opportunities to explore real and imaginary situations involving turn-taking, considering how these incidences can be resolved.

Suggestions Box

Practitioners should be mindful of the powerful emotions children may experience when turn-taking (anger, frustration, disappointment, hatred). Ensure they know how to vent these emotions in 'suitable' ways to prevent others being physically or verbally harmed!

54. Magpies in the classroom! Children who steal things

I am very uneasy about doing PPA in one class because there is a child who steals things. He has taken children's snacks from their bags, toys from their drawers, and has even been found taking money out of the class teacher's purse. The worrying thing he is only six! How can I manage this behaviour when I am in class with him?

Higher Level Teaching Assistant

When any child is found to have stolen something it becomes a concern for practitioners, the school and the child's parents. Fear, embarrassment and anger are common feelings associated with finding out or hearing that children you work with are prone to stealing other people's belongings. We should, however, take a moment to reflect on the following:

> **Points to note**
> ◆ Rarely do children reach adulthood without taking something which does not belong to them. It is normal for a very young child to take something which is interesting or exciting even though it does not belong to him/her. It is classed as stealing though if a child continues to do this from the age of three upwards.
> ◆ Parents/carers and practitioners are a role model for children. If you take stationery from work or do not pay for something you take out of a shop by mistake then you are stealing!

The first step in managing this behaviour is to work out the underlying reasons behind why the child is stealing.

> **Activity**
> Overleaf is a list of potential reasons why children steal. Read these and then order them in terms of which reasons you feel are applicable to the age of children you work with (1 being the most predominant reason). Reflect on previous experiences you have had with children stealing to help you.

Comfort

Impress others – supposed 'friends'

Get back at peers or adults – act of revenge

Have things they want – only way to get it

Feelings of excitement – surge of adrenaline

Give items as presents to others

Seeking attention – from peers and adults

For money – support drug habit

Think they can get away with it – not learned to respect the rights of others

Children in the early years usually steal because they want to have things that other children have got. Even though they have the developmental maturity to know what does and does not belong to them, many may not have developed the self-discipline to actually restrain themselves. Other reasons may be applicable but these are in extreme cases and are more related to older children and teenagers.

Reflection time

◆ How did your ordering activity compare to ideas presented above?

◆ Which of the reasons has helped you to understand why children in your class may be stealing?

Once you have the 'reason' you now have to select the most appropriate way to manage the behaviour. Best practice is summarized in three easy steps:

When dealing with a situation you should address it in a straightforward and compassionate way.

2. Speak about your concerns and directly state what must be done to rectify the situation.
3. Consider what the child should do if the situation happens again.

It is human nature to feel some negative emotions towards a child who has stolen from you or others, but as a professional you should avoid using any of the following approaches:

◆ losing your temper – this could act as a reward for them;
◆ encouraging children to lie their way out of the situation;
◆ argue with a child if she claims she has not taken something which you know she has;
◆ lecturing them at great length – they will quickly stop listening;
◆ holding a grudge after the incident.

Good practice in managing this behaviour is shown when:

◆ the child is not labelled by his behaviour – such as being called 'Tea leaf' (rhyming slang for thief);
◆ parents/carers are involved in supporting the child at home – 'a partnership for prevention';
◆ practitioners practise what they preach! (I am not accusing you of being a thief though!).

Top Tips!
◆ Always promote honesty in the classroom. Use everyday events – stories from the television/school – as a starting point for talking about honesty, integrity and family morals.
◆ Reward acts of honesty.
◆ Encourage the children to do the right thing. It might not be the easy thing to do but it means that the situation is put right.
◆ Prevention is better than cure – lock up your belongings (in your cupboards or desk) and encourage the children to leave items of value at home.

55. *Pickity Pick Pick!* Nose picking in class!

I can cope with most things but nose picking is just not one of them! I work with a couple of boys who always appear to have their finger up their nose! I plan for activities which mean they need to use their hands but as soon as I explain what they have to do – whoosh! – a finger begins to probe their nostrils! What can I do about this?

Nursery practitioner

Nose picking in both children and adults is generally frowned on in public and by society as a whole as it is perceived to be a disgusting bad habit. However, most of us actually do it, regardless of gender, age and cultural background. Nose picking in children is a very common 'act', so it is important for all practitioners to have an understanding of this behaviour to be able to manage it effectively.

Find Out!

♦ How many children in your class pick their noses during a lesson/session? Use other practitioners, parent helpers or your 'eagle' eyes to count how many children do this.

♦ Compare your results with a class further up the school or lower down – how do the results compare? Why do you think this is the case?

♦ Talk with other practitioners about why they think that children pick their noses. What do they do to prevent children doing this?

♦ Make a note of the key points which come out of these discussions and compare them with the rest of the information relating to this behaviour.

While this is not a pleasant topic for discussion there are different types of nose picking which practitioners should be aware of:

♦ Innocent – exploration of the face with the fingers (particularly noted in babies and young children).
Occasional – removal of a crust of nasal secretion (bogies) which may be obstructing, hurting, itching or hanging out of the nose.
Compulsive – pulling out of nasal hairs.

◆ Harmful – cause of frequent nose bleeds by picking too hard or too deep with objects or contaminated fingers.

Point to note

Nose picking may be an indication that a child is suffering from worms, a disease or a compulsive disorder. Children who suffer from the above may need to be seen by a doctor or a psychologist.

Children pick their nose for a number of reasons:

◆ trying to attract attention from peers and adults;
◆ boredom;
◆ itching or uncomfortable bogies;
◆ deliberate attempt to embarrass adults.

Practitioners should be mindful of these when considering the best way to manage the behaviour. Ways to do this include:

◆ Don't panic! Keep calm and avoid making a big issue out of it.
◆ Use non-verbal strategies – raise an eyebrow, shake your head as a negative, use your 'practitioner glare' or slow stare to stop the child.
◆ Encourage children to bring a handkerchief with them to the setting every day.
◆ Give children something to do with their hands – hold a white-board and pen, sing 'finger fun' songs, fold arms, sit on hands, use a number fan.
◆ Have a ready supply of tissues available for children to wipe their noses as and when necessary.
◆ Have a chat about the act of nose picking to a 'nose picker' on a one-to-one basis. If the issue persists talk to the class as a whole during circle time/PSHCE about their feelings and ideas relating to this topic.
◆ Speak to parents/carers about your concerns. See if the issue has been noted in the home environment.
◆ Make a joke out of the situation. Use phrases such as 'Any gold up there?', 'If you don't stop that your head will cave in!' or 'I see you're trying to scratch that itch in your brain!'

Considerations and Top Tips!

◆ Children may pick their noses if the atmosphere is too dry as a result of air conditioning or excessive heat. Mucus in the nose will dry up, thus forming the bogies which children will want to pick.

◆ Make children aware of the importance of mucus and hairs up the nose – these are used to trap dust and dirt which may be in the air to prevent damage to the respiratory system.

◆ Always encourage children to wipe or blow their noses rather than snorting mucus out – high pressure can damage delicate parts of the nose.

56. Parp! Fuuuuuut! Bhhrrrrrr!
Sounds and smells in the classroom

One child in the class I work with suffers from excessive flatulence. It never ceases to cause the rest of the class to smirk and giggle when they hear him pass wind but then it takes ages for them to calm down after that. The real issue is the smell which accompanies the 'sound' which at times is pretty vile; once it was so bad we had to go and work outside. What can I do about this?

Year 4 Teaching Assistant

Without going into *too* much detail practitioners should remember that everyone passes gas; it is a natural part of being a human being. With this in mind breaking wind (or 'farting' as it is commonly known) is not a bad behaviour. There are few health risks associated with flatulence, it is just a matter of children and adults being able to accept and control certain aspects of it.

All of the behaviours explored in this book consider the underlying reasons as to why these behaviours happen. While most of us have a basic understanding of why flatulence occurs (it's all about food, right?) a more scientific explanation can be found at www.askme.com/sports/health/38_mens_health.html if readers wish to find out more about digestive enzymes, unabsorbed nutrients and the 'oh-so-nasty' hydrogen sulphide.

Flatulent foods . . . or are they?

One of the main causes of flatulence is linked to certain foods people eat (although they do not apply to everybody). Look at the foods below and tick those you believe would cause flatulence in children:

☐ apples   ☐ carrots   ☐ pears
☐ apricots   ☐ cauliflower   ☐ peppers
☐ aubergine   ☐ dairy products   ☐ popcorn
☐ beans   ☐ button mushrooms   ☐ prunes
☐ bran   ☐ fish   ☐ raisins
☐ broccoli   ☐ nuts   ☐ soya beans
☐ brussels sprouts ☐ onions   ☐ tuna
☐ cabbage   ☐ peaches   ☐ watermelon

Dietetic foods, sugar-free sweets and gum, soft drinks, fatty foods including chips and whole grains (bread) are also 'flatulent culprits', so to speak. For the answers please refer to the end of this section.

Interestingly, there are other reasons as to why some children suffer more from flatulence than others. These include:

◆   being lactose intolerant;
◆   drinking through a straw;
◆   swallowing too much air, usually caused by chewing gum or by nervous habit;
◆   suffering an overgrowth of bacteria in the colon.

Warning! Excessive flatulence may be a symptom of a serious health problem such as appendicitis, gallstones, a stomach ulcer and/or irritable bowel syndrome. Children should never be encouraged to hold wind in for long periods of time as this can cause damage to their bowels and intestines.

So, what should we as practitioners do to effectively manage the 'sounds' and 'smells' which inevitably will be produced in every classroom across the country?

◆ Do join in with the laughter for a little while if it is a 'one off' incident, after all you are only human!
◆ Strategically ignore it.
◆ Politely ask the child if he needs to go to the toilet.
◆ Discourage other children from 'holding their noses' and dramatically 'wafting their hands across their faces'.
◆ Ask the child to sit near the classroom door, so if she needs to leave the room at any time she will not disturb others.
◆ If it is a regular occurrence try, wherever possible, not to laugh as it will set other children off.
◆ Ensure the child has regular opportunities to run outside to get some 'fresh air'.
◆ Encourage the child to drink carbonated drinks in moderation to juices, water and squash.
◆ Talk to the class as a whole about the need for us all to break wind but for it to be done in an appropriate manner.
◆ Encourage the child to go to the toilet before he comes into the classroom for each lesson.

To prevent the behaviour becoming a constant issue, practitioners are recommended to use the following strategies:

◆ Talk to parents/carers about the kinds of food the child is eating at home/school and the foods which will cause flatulence.
◆ Work together to ensure her diet is relatively free of gassy foods.
◆ Encourage parents/carers to prepare suitable foods for the child to bring if having a packed lunch or a special class picnic.
◆ Encourage the child to select certain foods from the school menu if having school dinners.
◆ Make the child aware of the foods he eats which cause him to have excessive wind. Encourage him to eat these foods in moderation.

Answers to Flatulent foods . . . or are they?
Everything on the chart except watermelon, fish and peppers!

Behaviours and whole-school events and occasions

57. Worth-ship? Children and collective worship

My class just do not seem to behave themselves during collective worship. They do not listen to the person delivering, nor do they sit properly, and I have seen many of them talking to each other when they should be singing. What can be done to manage these behaviours?

Year 1 teacher

Collective worship is a statutory part of school life, yet it can be a particularly uncomfortable time for some practitioners who may spend most of their time 'eyeballing' children in their class who are behaving inappropriately during it.

From Foundation Two children to the Year 6 class, no one is safe from the temptation to 'switch off' and either talk, play with people's hair, aggravate those nearby by poking and prodding them or singing in a silly voice (or not singing at all). Many practitioners observe the behaviours of children in other classes in their school and compare these to that of their own class – it can be embarrassing and disheartening if your class come bottom of the best behaved list!

Reflective questions

♦ How would you say your class fares with other classes in the school with regard to behaviour during collective worship?

♦ Do you have many behavioural issues during collective worship with your particular class?

♦ Why do you think this is the case?

♦ What strategies do you use to manage these behaviours?

♦ Which of these strategies do you use before they go into collective worship, during and after it?

Many behavioural issues relating to collective worship are a result of the following:

♦ Timing – afternoon collective worship does not have the same impact as worship undertaken in the morning.

♦ Boredom – content is meaningless/inappropriate to the children, delivery is slow and lacking in pace, the 'same sort of thing' happens every day.

♦ Temperature – warm/cold halls have an effect on the attention span of the children sitting in them.

♦ Practitioners – many practitioners do not model good behaviours during collective worship, either by not attending or sitting marking books, or not listening to the delivery.

♦ Duration – collective worship may run over into children's valuable playtime.

♦ Leader – the adult delivering the collective worship does not know how to communicate with children or is ill-prepared.

Managing the behaviour of children is difficult for those leading collective worship as they may be external speakers who have limited experiences of delivering to children, or practitioners who are able to manage their own class of 30 children yet find three, possibly four hundred children slightly more of a challenge!

Collective worship can be managed using a 'threefold' approach:

Before	During	After
♦ As the children line up remind them of behaviours you expect of them.	♦ Make a mental/written note of well-behaved children and those misbehaving.	♦ Speak to the children about their behaviour after collective worship.
♦ Ensure they walk in silence to collective worship – set the standard of behaviour straight-away.	♦ Move children who are not behaving appropriately.	♦ Use school reward systems to praise good behaviour.
♦ Use circle time opportunities to discuss appropriate behaviours for collective worship.	♦ Praise children who are listening and contributing to collective worship through non-verbal strategies.	♦ Keep children behind who have not behaved themselves – use sanctions to punish these children.
	♦ Give stickers for good behaviour.	

Top Tips!

There are a number of top tips practitioners can adopt as effective practice to ensure poor behaviour does not interfere with collective worship:

◆ Have quiet music playing as the children come into the hall. Ask the children questions about the music once everyone is settled – how well were they listening?
◆ Use drama and storytelling techniques to engage the children during collective worship.
◆ Always have stimulating resources to capture the interest and imagination of those listening to you, e.g. hats, cloaks and masks.
◆ Avoid reading straight from a book.
◆ Plan for the children to be actively involved, either where they are sat or as individuals brought to the front of the hall (asking questions, taking on the role of a character).
◆ Ensure the subject content is appropriate for the age of the children to whom you are delivering. Wherever possible relate learning to their lives (present/future).
◆ Use the internet to download creative ideas and approaches to liven up collective worship.
◆ Invite external speakers to talk to the children. Talk to other schools about speakers they use for quality assurance.
◆ Sing your heart out when singing the song/hymn.

58. 'I've come in today to talk to you about . . . ' Visiting guest speakers

I like inviting guest speakers into my school yet I am always embarrassed . . . no, ashamed of the behaviour of some of the children in the hall when the guests are speaking. I seem to always apologize to the speakers when they leave, saying 'They are not normally like that'! Truth is they usually are! How can I make sure the children actually listen and behave themselves?

Headteacher, large primary school

Guest speakers are a wonderful way to bring new knowledge, experiences, ideas and thinking to life, particularly as they are a 'new face' for the children to see during the school day. There is a whole range of different speakers which schools can utilize to support learning and teaching:

- Parents / grandparents
- Local vicar / priest / nun
- Representatives – charities, coaching courses
- Services – police, fire, ambulance
- Theatre groups
- Orchestras
- Local celebrities – radio, TV
- Storytellers.

While there are many benefits to bringing them into school there are also many potential issues, most of them relating to the children's behaviour, when the guest speaker is faced, if in the hall, with 300+ children.

Reflective questions
- How often do you have guest speakers in your school?
- What behavioural issues do you find when they speak to a class/the school?
- Why do you think this is the case?
- What do you do to support the guest speaker/manage the children's behaviour?

As the children's poor behaviour can give guests 'the wrong impression' as to how well the school is teaching the children to behave, it is important to consider not only ways to manage this situation but also to understand why the children misbehave:

- attention seeking;
- children know speaker is not a trained practitioner – children do not respect them;
- bored – lack of interaction and engagement;
- topic of discussion is too complicated / simple for those listening – not pitched at the right level;
- relevance of speaker is unknown – children do not understand why they have come in to talk to them;
- talk is very longwinded and lacking in pace / focus;
- speaker talks for too long and 'eats' into the children's playtime;
- speaker overstimulates the children with, for example, music or magic;
- children are tired.

There are a number of warning signs practitioners should look out for when guest speakers are delivering as they usually indicate that the children's behaviour is about to deteriorate:

◆ restlessness – lots of fidgeting / fiddling;
◆ children not looking at the guest speaker;
◆ turning around;
◆ whispering to others;
◆ playing with hair and shoe laces;
◆ uncrossing legs;
◆ sighing;
◆ eyes closed;
◆ slouching.

Strategies offered to manage and prevent this behaviour from occurring relate not only to the children and school but also to the guest speaker which practitioners are encouraged to share and use:

Children/school	Guest speakers
◆ Use PHSCE and circle time opportunities to talk about desirable behaviours with guest speakers. ◆ Practise behaviours before speakers come to school. ◆ Remind children of high expectations. ◆ Have rules displayed around the hall. ◆ Use your practitioner 'glare'. ◆ Position troublesome children at the end of the line. ◆ Give awards to good listeners/well-behaved classes. ◆ Ensure there are practitioners in the hall to keep children under control.	◆ Make sure they are well prepared – ensure they do not just 'blag it' or read from a book. ◆ Only use speakers who work with other schools for quality assurance purposes. ◆ Talk to them on the phone – do they have an engaging voice? ◆ Offer them simple strategies to manage children's behaviour if required. ◆ Ensure they deliver what you need them to (age and content appropriate). ◆ Set time limits – give five and two-minute warnings. ◆ Encourage interaction –

◆ Play calming music when the children enter/leave the hall.

◆ Allow children to have a quick run around on the playground before they come into the hall.

◆ Set children a challenge – try to remember three things said – test the children when they return to class.

◆ Remove children if being disruptive.

questions, comments, participation.

◆ Promote use of visual aids to support delivery – OHT, puppets, pictures.

◆ Allow them to come and see you talk to the children – model practice.

One school I know uses a wonderful little strategy; the guest speaker is allowed to select one class they feel who has been the best behaved to go out first and have two extra minutes play. Unsurprisingly all the children are very well-behaved when they are in!

59. Musical Madness! Whole-school singing practice

I am the music co-ordinator at school and part of my role is to ensure the children sing hymns and songs to the best of their ability during collective worship, special assemblies and the Christmas and Easter festivals. I find it a real battle to get the children to concentrate during singing practice and give it their all – what can I do to ensure their behaviour does not let their singing down?

Year 5 teacher, music co-ordinator

Hearing children sing together as a whole school is a wonderful experience and it is extremely rewarding for any practitioner who is enthusiastic/musical/brave (!) enough to undertake the job of teaching them to sing in unison.

Find Out!

◆ Who does singing practice with the whole school? Why do they do it?

◆ When is it done during the school week? Why is it done then?

◆ What support is given to the practitioner during the practice? Who is involved in providing this support?

◆ How is the children's behaviour managed during this time? Are there any strategies used to pre-empt certain behaviours?

◆ What strategies could you adopt as part of your own practice?

Most children enjoy singing and relish the opportunity to sing along with their peers and other children in the school. As singing in most schools is an integral feature of daily school life, singing practice, or 'hymn practice' as it is known, is important to ensure the children are taught the tuneful melodies, the correct words they are to read and recite, and use the appropriate dynamics, tone and phrasing to ensure it is pleasing on the ears of anyone fortunate enough to hear the children sing.

However, few children like the notion of having to practise something and, as a result, the following behaviours are usually exhibited when the school practises together:

◆ fidgeting and restlessness;
◆ children not taking part;
◆ bored expressions;
◆ lethargic body language;
◆ sighing;
◆ children talking to those either side of them;
◆ being silly;
◆ singing too quietly, too loudly or unenthusiastically;
◆ lack of general attentiveness and interest;
◆ singing rude or the wrong words.

Why oh why oh why?

Take a moment to reflect on the behaviours identified on page 189 and make a note of one reason for each which you can think of that explains why a child may behave in that way. Focus your thinking either on one specific class or key stage.

While it is not possible for us to explore every behaviour listed above, the notion of children not taking part is interesting for a number of reasons:

1. Boys are more reluctant to sing as they do not perceive it to be a 'manly' thing to do.
2. Children in Years 5 and 6 become reticent to join in as they become very self-conscious about their own abilities and feel it is somewhat 'beneath them' and rather 'silly'.
3. Some children in Foundation Two and Year One struggle to read and learn all the words to songs and so find it hard to make a contribution.

An abundance of strategies is available which not only manage behaviour during the singing practice but also pre-empt it from occurring.

Before, during or both?

Read the strategies below and indicate by the side of each one whether you would use it before the practice begins (B), during the session (D) or both (B/D). An example has been done for you.

- State expectations of behaviour. B/D
- Praise good behaviour seen. ____
- Share the purpose of the session with the children. ____
- Use children to model good singing. ____
- Select songs which cater for different interests. ____
- Model enthusiasm for singing. ____

- ◆ Vary the way the children sing – quietly, loudly, in a robotic voice. ____

- ◆ Teach songs slowly line by line, verse by verse. ____

- ◆ Select songs for just EYFS, KS1 and KS2 to sing. ____

- ◆ Choose songs with meaning to the children. ____

- ◆ Put words up on an OHT to prevent voices becoming muffled by hymnbooks held over their mouths. ____

- ◆ Challenge the school – Is KS1 better than KS2? Are the boys better than the girls? ____

- ◆ Award team points/stickers to individuals and classes for exceptional effort and behaviour. ____

- ◆ Select songs with humour and actions. ____

- ◆ Allow the children to select songs for the school to learn/sing. ____

- ◆ Use other practitioners as crowd control. ____

- ◆ Sing with the piano, CD accompaniment and unaccompanied. ____

60. Class assemblies and the children who do not take any notice of them

It takes a lot of time and effort to make a class assembly work and I am always very proud of my children's efforts when it is all over! I feel, however, that the rest of the school do not seem to pay any attention to them and I become very angry when I see children in the 'audience' talking and messing about. What can be done to manage this behaviour?

Year 3 teacher

It is quite understandable for emotions to run high when a class of children and practitioners who work with them put in hours of hard work to produce an exciting and interesting class assembly and then for the rest of the school to not pay any attention to it at all.

> **Do remember:**
> ◆ It is not the whole school who are not listening – it is usually only a few children.
> ◆ Practitioners and children become very emotional when preparing for and leading a class assembly due to the amount of effort and energy needed to make it a success – try to not take it too much to heart!

Class assemblies are wonderful opportunities to share children's current learning with the rest of the school and parents / carers who come to see it. It is always a joy to see children showing new skills, knowledge and understanding they have acquired to others and this is a perfect opportunity for practitioners to step back (if only for a moment!) and evaluate just how effective they are.

Clearly though it is very disappointing for the children leading the assembly to be faced with the rest of the school and for them to seemingly not pay any attention to it.

>
> **Find Out!**
> During the next class assembly in your school take a few moments to observe the 'audience' of children. Consider why they are attentive at times during it and why they 'switch off' and pay less attention to the assembly at other times.

Behaviours which are common during class assemblies include:

◆ talking to others;
◆ looking around the hall;
◆ turning around;
◆ fidgeting;
◆ playing with their own or other children's hair;
◆ sighing;
◆ restlessness;
◆ poking and prodding others;
◆ looking down at the floor.

These behaviours can be very off-putting for children who are nervous enough at having to perform in front of the whole school and all the parents sat at the back of the room. Knowing why children behave in these ways is useful for practitioners so they can put strategies in place to prevent them from occurring. These include the audience:

◆ not being able to hear those speaking;
◆ not understanding what is going on or what is being said;
◆ not being able to see all the children;
◆ not having an active part to play – they are just expected to sit and listen;
◆ becoming bored with the same sort of delivery – one child stands up and talks, the next child stands up and talks. . . .

Turning the negatives into positives

Rewrite the bullet points above into a series of positive action points you could plan for and share with your class to ensure the rest of the school remain attentive while their class assembly is being performed.

◆
_____

◆
_____

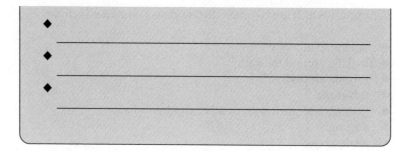

There are ways to ensure children do pay attention to the class assembly:

◆ Allow all the children to have a quick run around outside before they come into the hall.

◆ Have a time when you wish to start and ensure everyone else is in the hall before that time (or have the class performing in place before the rest of the school arrives).

◆ Ask practitioners to remind their class about expected behaviours in the hall before they leave their classroom.

◆ Refer to the wall display on 'hall rules' when all the children are settled.

◆ Ask practitioners to monitor their class's behaviour during the assembly.

◆ Ask practitioners to ask their class questions about the assembly after they have seen it (not just 'did you enjoy that?'!)

Quality class assemblies have certain features which never fail to keep children's interest:

◆ children playing musical instruments (made / real);
◆ drama;
◆ dance;
◆ singing;
◆ audience participation – chanting repeated phrases, clapping, hand actions;
◆ costumes;
◆ props;
◆ scenery;
◆ pictures;
◆ items the children have made;
◆ humour;
◆ movement – gymnastic displays.

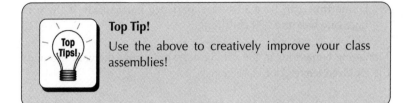

Top Tip!
Use the above to creatively improve your class assemblies!

61. Food, glorious food! Dinnertime in schools

I am glad that I do not have to manage the behaviour of some of the children in our school during dinnertime! They seem to go absolutely wild as soon as the bell rings at midday! The problem is we have to deal with incidents when the children come back to us at one o'clock. What can I do about this?

Year 3 teacher

In most schools dinnertime is a noisy, frantic and busy time during which food is dropped on the floor, drinks are spilt, children run to tables to sit next to their friends and voices are much louder than are actually necessary.

Find Out!
How does the behaviour of your class change from being in your classroom to being in the dining hall? Observe your class for about ten minutes from when you finish teaching at midday to them eating their dinner. Make a note of the ways in which the children 'change'

There is always a marked difference in children's behaviour when they go in the hall for dinner for the following reasons:

◆ Practitioners are not around.
◆ Children have less respect for midday supervisors.
◆ Midday supervisors find it difficult to manage children's behaviour (they are not trained practitioners).
◆ Children forget that behaviours in the playground should not be brought into the dining hall.

♦ Dinnertime can be a rushed experience particularly if there is only one hall and 300 children.

Managing behaviour in the dining hall starts from the very moment the children leave your classroom:

♦ Ensure all children have been to the toilet and washed their hands before they leave.
♦ Ensure all children are lined up 'straight and silent' before they leave.
♦ Expect all children to *walk* down the corridor and into the hall. Stop children who run and send them back to the classroom to 'try again'.
♦ Set your class challenges with the midday supervisor, e.g. 'When you come back after dinner, I want Mrs Johnson to be able to tell me at least six children who have been brilliant in the dinner hall today, okay?'

Once in the hall:

♦ Play calming music in the background.
♦ Regularly eat your dinner with the children; model how to sit, use your knife and fork, chat and eat with your mouth closed!
♦ If appropriate ask the children to say a silent prayer to say thanks for their food before they begin eating.
♦ Teach the children to not leave their seats until they have finished their food; always ask them to push their chairs under after them.
♦ Encourage the children to talk to their neighbours and not shout across the table/hall.
♦ Expect the children to put up their hands if they need a packet opening or a spillage mopping up.
♦ Remind the children to use their manners.
♦ Have the headteacher/deputy make spot checks to assess how well-behaved the children are being.

Case Study

One primary school found that the children's behaviour in the dining hall was slowly deteriorating. As action needed to be taken the headteacher discussed the issues with the Year 6 class and together they devised a rota which allowed children in the class who wished to be involved to act as 'dinner monitors'. Their role involved them observing different classes eating, helping to clear plates and noting how calm the children were during their allotted time in the dining hall. At the end of each dinnertime the monitors would get together and award each class 'dinnertime points' which would be added together at the end of the week and shared with the whole school during the awards assembly. The class with the highest score would be able to go into the hall for dinner first the following week. The competitive atmosphere suddenly made dinnertime in the school a much calmer and safer time!

To prevent dinnertime being an issue for schools, a number of long-term approaches for effective management are available:

◆ Work with midday supervisors to develop and consistently use appropriate rewards and sanctions.
◆ Invite midday supervisors to attend LA behaviour management training.
◆ Devise school rules for the dining hall and display these.
◆ Develop a whole-school policy linked to dinnertime in consultation with kitchen staff, midday supervisors and staff.
◆ Use PSHCE, circle time and assemblies to discuss issues and behaviours in the dining hall.

62. 'They speak to me like muck!' Children's behaviours towards midday supervisors

I like my job but some of the children are just plain rude. I don't deserve to be shouted at by anyone, especially children. I'm not a teacher and I don't get their pay but I am there to ensure the children are safe during the dinner hour and it makes me angry when they think they can talk to me like a piece of dirt!

Midday supervisor, Year 6

Midday supervisors do a difficult job during a particularly hectic part of the school day. While many of them have children of their own, midday supervisors do not have the skills to effectively manage a class of 30+ children, particularly if they are all hungry and desperate to get on to the playground.

Many children across the age phases recognize that midday supervisors are not trained practitioners and do not usually show them the level of courtesy and respect they deserve. Behaviours usually exhibited therefore include children forgetting their manners, shouting, beckoning orders to open packets of food for them, or ignoring requests for them to push their chairs under or clear their plates away.

Have a 'little chat'

Talk to your midday supervisor. Ask them to make a list of the behaviours they deal with on a daily basis specific to your class. Make your own list and compare the two – how similar/different are they?

There are other reasons as to why children do not treat midday supervisors appropriately:

◆ general lack of respect for any adults;
◆ midday supervisor does not treat the children fairly or appropriately;
◆ children get caught up in the 'freedom' for an hour during dinner time and forget to behave.

Case Study

A midday supervisor for a Year 4 class had children not only spitting and swearing at her, but also ignoring her requests, calling her names and pulling silly faces behind her back, laughing at her, and refusing to sit down when they were eating. The midday supervisor spoke to her colleagues and tried some different strategies to manage the children but they all failed. She eventually discussed these issues with the class teacher but things just seemed to get worse. In desperation the midday supervisor spoke to the headteacher who said that he was '. . . too busy' to deal with the situation. She eventually left the job due to stress.

Reflect on the above and consider what you would do differently to support the midday supervisor in this situation.

To effectively manage this behaviour strategies need to be specific to both the children and the midday supervisors.

Copy, cut, sort and stick!

Photocopy the strategy cards below. Cut them out and use the chart provided overleaf to organize them into specific strategies for children and midday supervisors.

Talk to the children about respecting other adults in school.	Invite the midday supervisor into class to talk to the children about his role/expectations.	Use PHSCE and circle time to talk about the feelings of midday supervisors.

Ask midday supervisors to come into class and support the children five minutes before dinnertime to ensure a smooth transition.

Follow up any behavioural issues midday supervisors make you aware of.

Allow midday supervisors to give stickers and certificates to children who are well-behaved.

Provide midday supervisors with lists of simple behaviour management strategies to help them in their role.

Eat your dinner with your class to monitor behaviours of both the children and the midday supervisors.

Use a class behaviour book which is completed by the midday supervisor every day, noting good and poor behaviours in the class.

Ask the children to identify how they would like their midday supervisor to be with them. Discuss appropriate requests with them.

Model management strategies for getting the children to be quiet or in a nice line for midday supervisors to see and use.

Remind the children of the school rules – which ones relate specifically to midday supervisors?

Praise children who are respectful of the midday supervisors.

Talk to the midday supervisor about what she can do to get the children 'on side'.

Review expectations regularly so midday supervisors/children know what is expected.

Midday supervisors	Children

There a number of top tips for preventing this behaviour:

◆ Establish clear expectations of behaviour between the children and midday supervisors right from the start of the year.
◆ Suggest midday supervisors attend courses run by the LA.
◆ Encourage midday supervisors to use the school's reward and sanction systems.
◆ Request midday supervisors to 'look for the good'!

63. Super or stressful Sports Day? Sports Day at school

Sports Day at school used to be great fun but now I hate it because of the behavioural issues associated with it. The worst part is the parents being there and watching us practitioners trying to manage the jeering, pushing and unpleasantness we seem to have to deal with from the children. How can we make Sports Day a little less stressful?

Year 4 teacher

Sports Day for most children is a great opportunity to show off their physical abilities as opposed to their academic skills. However, this special occasion in the school calendar is also a time for poor sportsmanship, aggressive competitiveness and unnecessary pressure to mar an afternoon of potential fun, enjoyment and excitement.

> **Do remind them!**
> Children need to be reminded that Sports Day is a time when they are representing not only themselves but also their school team and their school as a whole. Sports Day should be memorable for all the right reasons!

While practitioners work hard to organize and run a successful Sports Day, they also have to deal effectively with certain behaviours exhibited by not only the children but also parents/carers!

Activity
Make a list of behaviours you have seen in parents at Sports Days you have either attended or been involved in. Compare these to the common behaviours noted in children during the sports afternoon:

◆ jeering;
◆ laughing at others for their 'poor' performance;
◆ tears, tantrums and potential fighting;
◆ pushing in the line;

◆ not listening to instructions;
◆ overexcitement;
◆ unpleasant or derogatory chanting.

How does your school attempt to manage parental behaviours on Sports Day?

So why do practitioners have to deal with more behavioural problems during Sports Day? Possible reasons include:

◆ Change in daily routine – some children cannot cope with this.
◆ Parental influence – children are 'told' to win.
◆ Pressure – from peers to perform well.
◆ Overexcitement – children like to go outside and do something different.
◆ Male bravado – boys particularly relish competition.

Suggestions Box

Children need to understand how competitiveness can become an unhealthy and unpleasant way of thinking/living if they do not learn how to manage it effectively.

◆ Ensure children know that while winning is nice, taking part is just as important.
◆ Encourage local sports people to speak to the school about how they manage feelings and thinking linked with competitiveness.

To effectively manage behaviours during Sports Day *preparation is the key to success.*

◆ As a whole school decide how you will organize the Sports Day – roles, responsibilities, groupings of children, activities. Ask the children for their ideas as well.
◆ Ensure adults are willing to work as a team in running the day –

a consistent, collaborative approach will help to ensure the day runs smoothly.

◆ Talk to the whole school during an assembly explaining what will be happening, how it will be organized and expectations of the children during the day.

◆ Teach the children to 'Cheer, not Jeer!'

◆ Provide the children with opportunities during playtime and PE sessions to practise Sports Day activities so that they feel comfortable with what they are expected to do.

◆ Undertake a 'practice' Sports Day to ensure all aspects of the day run smoothly. If things do not go to plan either adapt your practice or get the children to practise parts of it again until it is right!

◆ Remind the children of rules and expectations just before they go out onto the field – a friendly 'word of warning' sometimes works wonders!

◆ Use PSHCE and circle time opportunities to talk about managing feelings of winning and losing.

The actual Sports Day . . .

◆ Have a whistle to hand if necessary.

◆ Use children from local secondary schools to help manage the children's behaviour and run activities.

◆ Ensure there are lots of activities for the children to be doing.

◆ Keep queues and waiting times for tasks to an absolute minimum.

◆ Ensure activities can be adapted for different ages/abilities.

◆ Ensure the children have access to water to keep them hydrated.

◆ Provide lots of encouragement and praise not only for achievement but also effort. Ensure awards, prizes and certificates reflect both aspects.

◆ Avoid sweets as treats – they will either get lost or the sugar rush may cause some children to get a little high.

Important advice

If children do not behave themselves during Sports Day do not compromise your expectations – remove the children from activities until they are prepared to behave.

64. End of the day mayhem! Children and hometime

The bell rings to indicate the end of the school day and my class suddenly seem to lose the plot! The noise level in the cloakroom is unbearable and so many children forget to collect reading bags, jumpers and lunchboxes that it can be 15:40 before all the children have completely gone! What can I do to ensure the children are calm and organized during this time?

Year 5 teacher

Hometime for virtually every school is a frantic five / ten minutes where every child in every class at the end of the day tries to gather their own personal belongings and rush out of the school gates all at the same time! It is inevitable that this time will be noisy, busy with movement and a 'race against time'. Or does it have to be . . . ?

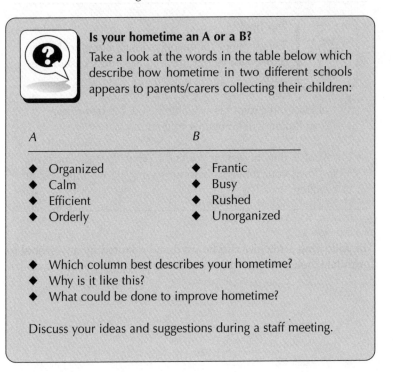

Is your hometime an A or a B?

Take a look at the words in the table below which describe how hometime in two different schools appears to parents/carers collecting their children:

A	B
◆ Organized	◆ Frantic
◆ Calm	◆ Busy
◆ Efficient	◆ Rushed
◆ Orderly	◆ Unorganized

◆ Which column best describes your hometime?
◆ Why is it like this?
◆ What could be done to improve hometime?

Discuss your ideas and suggestions during a staff meeting.

It is important that your hometime is more like list A as opposed to list B as there is the potential for:

◆ Children to get hurt (kicked by accident, trampled fingers) in the rush to collect their things.
◆ Items to be taken in haste by children to whom they do not belong.
◆ Children to forget to take items, e.g. lunch boxes, inhalers and important letters.
◆ Parents/carers to become increasingly frustrated with their child coming out of school late.
◆ Parents/carers and practitioners becoming fed up with children having to rush back into school to collect items they have left.

Top Tips!

To pre-empt poor behaviours being exhibited during hometime practitioners must ensure they have:

1. at least three minutes available before the bell rings;
2. a well-planned 'hometime routine'.

But what is this 'hometime routine'? What does it consist of? Note down your thoughts before you engage with the rest of this section.

The following strategies can be used and adapted by any school to formulate their own hometime routine to pre-empt poor behaviours.

Rank, order and implement!

Rank the strategies in terms of their usefulness to you and your class (1 being the most useful, 9 being the least useful).

☐ Ask two children to act as noise monitors to assess how quietly the rest of the children can collect their things.

☐ Send children out in small groups as opposed to the entire class all at the same time. Vary the groups each day – girls, then boys, children with brown hair, green eyes . . .

☐ Assign children in the class different jobs to help you – one child to fold the jumpers up, one to collect any items left in the cloakroom, one to hand out the water bottles, one to hand out letters, one to hand out homework. . . .

☐ Award children team points and stickers for the quickest/ quietest in terms of collecting their things.

☐ Talk to the children about your expectations of their behaviours before they leave the classroom.

☐ Only allow the children to leave the school as a whole class when every child is ready to go.

☐ Verbally give out a checklist to ensure everyone has everything he or she should have, e.g. 'Coat?' 'YES!' 'Reading bag?' 'YES!'

☐ Use specific children to model how to get their things in a quiet and orderly fashion.

☐ Use a stop watch to time the children how long it takes to collect their things. Remind them that this is not a race – it is just a way to challenge the children to not waste time.

Top Tips!

◆ Encourage parents/carers to ensure everything the children bring to school has their name in it/on it.

◆ Most children try to put everything into their reading bag. Research has found this is affecting children's balance and body alignment. Encourage them to hold items in both their hands.

◆ Always remind children to come back if the person who comes to collect them is not there – 'Never go home with strangers'.

◆ Stagger classes leaving their classrooms to avoid a mass of children trying to get out of the one door.

9 | Behaviours and educational needs

65. Selective mutism in the classroom

I have worked hard to bring more speaking and listening into the classroom as I really value the development of these essential skills. I have one child, however, whom I know is able to talk yet will not open her mouth in large group/whole class activities. How can I help her to overcome this rather persistent behaviour as it is making it difficult for me to assess her speaking skills?

Year 2 teacher

Formally known as elective mutism, selective mutism is a complex anxiety disorder characterized by a child's lack of speech in at least one social context over a one month period or more. It is important to note that these children do understand language and are able to talk normally in situations where they are comfortable, secure and relaxed, i.e. in the home. Selective mutism affects approximately 1 per cent of children under the age of five years yet is noticeable when the child enters full-time schooling.

Reflective questions
- ◆ Does the information above relate to the child you are trying to support in your class?
- ◆ In what contexts are they anxious/relaxed? How do you know this?
- ◆ Apart from not speaking, how else do you know the child has a phobia about speaking to/in front of others?
- ◆ How does this make you feel?

This fear of speaking and of social interactions/events where there is an expectation to talk results in certain behaviours being exhibited. This not only includes their lips remaining 'tightly sealed' but also:

◆ keeping little to no eye contact with others;
◆ standing or sitting motionless;
◆ having a slight redness to the face – sign of embarrassment;
◆ 'freezing' suddenly;
◆ chewing/twirling their hair;
◆ biting their lip;
◆ exhibiting blank facial expressions;
◆ failing to smile with/at others;
◆ experiencing vomiting, diarrhoea and/or headaches.

Selective mutism in children is a potentially harmful behaviour as it interferes with their ability to function in an educational and/or social setting. These children may find it difficult to form friendships with others and may be branded by their peers as 'rude' and 'obnoxious' as they seem to ignore other people's attempts to communicate with them. This can lead to teasing and bullying issues. In many cases, however, classmates may take on a rather more protective role and try to speak for these children yet this clearly stifles their social growth and cognitive development.

Practitioners, as ever, are only in a position to manage this behaviour if they are aware of the reasons as to why a child will develop selective mutism.

Activity
Using a highlighter pen indicate the reasons which you think relate to why children develop selective mutism:

◆ inherited tendency from various family members;
◆ expressive language disorder;
◆ bilingual environments;
◆ stressful environment.

It is likely that you will have read this short list and thought to yourself 'What about the effects of abuse, neglect or trauma?' There is no evidence to support the idea that selective mutism is related to these factors even though it is still believed by many today.

Important to remember!
If a child remains mute for a number of years it can become a difficult habit to break as they may begin to believe that they will never be able to speak in certain settings or to certain individuals. It can lead to underachievement, depression and even crime. Early diagnosis and treatment is 'key' to helping the child overcome this disorder.

Assessments and treatments are varied and potentially involve a combination of the following therapies undertaken by trained professionals:

♦ behavioural;
♦ cognitive behavioural;
♦ play;
♦ psychoanalytical;
♦ medication;
♦ family.

Wonderful website!
For explicit details regarding how these therapies work, please refer to www.selectivemutism.org.

But what can practitioners do to support children in the classroom (as undertaking their own little 'therapy session' is not an option!)?

♦ Undertake some research on mutism.
♦ Remove all pressure and expectations for the child to speak.

- Empathize with the child.
- Ensure the child knows you understand that she feels 'scared' when she has to talk.
- Avoid bribing the child to speak.
- Reassure the child, telling him you will help him through this difficult time.
- Praise the child's achievements whenever possible.
- Offer support when the child becomes frustrated or anxious – 'Calm!' 'Breathe!'
- Offer the child opportunities to communicate when she wants to in different ways – verbal and non-verbal.

66. Children with Asperger Syndrome

I have a boy in my class who fascinates me. While being academically bright, his ability to form relationships with his peers is literally non-existent! He just does not seem to know how to connect with others in any social context yet give him a map and he can talk to whoever will listen for hours (literally!). How can I support this boy?

Year 5 teacher

Even though there is a lot of ongoing research into Asperger Syndrome, information relating to it is still limited particularly due to the fact that it is not easily diagnosed.

Reflection time!
What do you know about Asperger Syndrome? List all the facts and pieces of knowledge you know below:

_____

_____

_____

_____

_____

Read the rest of this section and put a tick by anything stated which you already knew. If you get to the end and find you have not ticked anything then please do not worry; it has been of great benefit for you to read this!

Asperger Syndrome is a neurological disorder which affects the ability for one to have appropriate social relationships. Children who suffer from Asperger Syndrome are quite bright and have great potential/ability to learn new things yet do not seem to be able to connect with other children socially. While there are not clinical delays in language or cognitive functioning, these children require lots of support and guidance to help them to function effectively in the classroom.

Find Out!

Fact: Some consider Asperger Syndrome to be a high functioning form of autism.

Fact: Some consider Asperger Syndrome to be its own unique disorder.

Dedicate a few moments to undertake an internet web search into Asperger Syndrome. Select six websites and scan the information provided.

Do more of the websites consider Asperger Syndrome to be a form of autism or a separate disorder?

Children with Asperger Syndrome are noticeable in the classroom due to the behaviours they show when working in any group or team context. As these children have no idea as to how to participate or co-operate and work together with others they will:

♦ talk non-stop;
♦ interrupt others unnecessarily;
♦ dominate;
♦ take no interest in what others have to say;

◆ show little empathy;
◆ be unable to take turns;
◆ have a poor attention span;
◆ engage with repetitive or irritating movements, e.g. clicking, tapping;
◆ not follow rules or routines – only talking when they are holding the 'Talking Stick' will just *not* happen;
◆ become obsessed about topics and subjects they particularly like;
◆ are blatantly truthful, e.g. 'You're fat!'

Case Study

James, a young boy in a Year 2 class, loved mathematics and could do calculations in his head almost at light speed! When it came to the oral and mental starters at the beginning of the numeracy sessions, James always had his hand up before any of the other children. As practitioners in the class wanted to ensure others had an opportunity to contribute, they would only let James answer a few questions. Increasingly frustrated by this, James began to laugh at others when they got the answer wrong, and would shout out the answers unnecessarily and stand up and scream if he was not chosen to give an answer. During independent work he would fill in children's worksheets if they were stuck or spend excessive amounts of time trying to explain to others how to calculate answers.

James had undiagnosed Asperger Syndrome.

Practitioners and the children in the class just thought he was very self-centred and unmanageable.

Children with Asperger Syndrome often exhibit unusual patterns of interest, e.g. age of trees, types of engines in trains, names of bodies of water. Practitioners are recommended to find out the interests of these children and integrate them into their planning, using them as 'knowledge experts' to support learning and teaching.

So how can we support the Year 5 practitioner who would like to help the boy who loves maps in her class? Well . . .

- Be patient with the child.
- Teach social skills regularly.
- Use a buddy system.
- Establish daily routines and try to stick to them.
- Inform children of any changes to routines well before they occur.
- Set a couple of simple rules for the child to follow.
- Keep stimuli and distractions in the class to a minimum.
- Allow them 'special interest time' to become absorbed in their field of interest.
- Use reward systems to help them to take turns and listen to others.

67. Children who suffer with dyspraxia

There is one child I work with whose physical movements are erratic to say the least! Even though he loves sports he finds it difficult to engage with PE sessions as he struggles to learn different skills and perform them with any care and thought. I am sure he is dyspraxic but I cannot be sure – can you help me?

Year 3 Teaching Assistant

Yes – I can help you! First, we need to ensure what dyspraxia actually is. Commonly referred to as an impairment or immaturity of the organization of movement, dyspraxia can affect one or more areas of development including language, perception and thought. The term normally used is Developmental Dyspraxia or Developmental Co-ordination Disorder (DCD).

Information for thought!
This condition is believed to affect up to 10 percent of the population in varying degrees of severity. It is likely that there is at least one dyspraxic child in every classroom – which child is it in your class?

Dyspraxia affects children in different ways and at different stages of their development. This means that establishing whether children have dyspraxia or not is difficult as their behaviours may be inconsistent in occurrence.

Are they or aren't they?

Take a moment to think about a child whom you think has dyspraxia in your class Does he suffer from:

- ◆ poor balance?
- ◆ poor posture and fatigue?
- ◆ poor hand–eye co-ordination?
- ◆ a lack of rhythm when dancing?
- ◆ a tendency to fall, trip or bump into things?
- ◆ a lack of manual dexterity?
- ◆ poor manipulation skills, e.g. writing and drawing?
- ◆ unclear speech?
- ◆ inability to sequence and structure stories?
- ◆ poor tracking of moving objects?
- ◆ little sense of time, speed, distance or weight?
- ◆ inadequate sense of direction?
- ◆ an inability to plan and organize things?
- ◆ poor memory?
- ◆ impulsiveness?
- ◆ stress?
- ◆ poor sleeping patterns?

Clearly many of these characteristics are not unique to people with dyspraxia yet many sufferers, who are more likely to be male than female, tend to have more than their fair share of co-ordination and perceptual difficulties. If the child in your class exhibits a number of these behaviours, he most likely has dyspraxia.

It is important to remember that the questions above are not a rigorous diagnosis tool – please use them to see if they 'fit' the child. Only specialists, including occupational therapists, speech and language therapists and psychologists are able to confirm whether a child has dyspraxia or not.

Many people ask the question 'What causes dyspraxia?' and the answer is simple – *there is no known cause*. Current thinking explores the possible immature development of the brain while the child is in the womb, while others question whether the brain is damaged by an illness, a stroke or an accident later in life.

Thinking Time!

How could dyspraxia potentially affect a child's ability to engage with the Early Years Foundation Stage curriculum/National Curriculum? Refer back to the questions on the Are they . . . or aren't they? task (page 216) and complete the appropriate chart below, highlighting aspects with which children with dyspraxia may struggle.

Children in the Early Years Foundation stage (3–5)

Area of learning	Potential difficulties
Personal, Social and Emotional Development	
Communication, Language and Literacy	
Problem solving, Calculating and Numeracy	
Knowledge and Understanding of the World	
Physical Development	

Creative Development	

Children in Primary Education (5–11)

National Curriculum subject area	*Potential difficulties*
English	
Mathematics	
Science	
ICT	
Humanities – Geography, History, Religious Education	
The Arts – Art and Design, Music, Dance, Drama	
Physical Education	

Design and Technology	
Modern Foreign Languages	
Personal, Social, Health and Citizenship Education	

While it is not possible to cure dyspraxia there are ways in which practitioners can help these children to learn ways to work around their difficulties so that they achieve their full potential. These include:

◆ working with specialist support to devise and implement strategies and programmes to build skills and achievement;
◆ supporting parents/carers with advice and exercises alongside specialist support;
◆ using practitioners or specialist support to give children one-to-one support when they need it;
◆ differentiating work to meet the child's favoured learning style;
◆ keeping instructions simple and to a minimum;
◆ ensuring work can be completed in the time given;
◆ recognizing children with dyspraxia will have 'good' and 'bad' days;
◆ praising children frequently to boost self-esteem and confidence;
◆ keeping teaching time short and succinct;
◆ setting realistic targets for them to achieve;
◆ have a 'back up' plan if the child becomes frustrated with his inability to perform an action or answer a question.

68. Managing children with autistic tendencies

There is something about a child in my class and I cannot put my finger on it but I think she is autistic. Please do not ask me why but . . . I just have this hunch that she is somewhere on the autistic spectrum due to the behaviours she exhibits. I really am at a loss as to what to do to help this child!

Year 1 teacher

Knowledge of the reader!

Clearly a 'hunch' is not enough for a practitioner to simply 'label' a child as being autistic. Use the space below to record all your knowledge about autism – what it is, what causes it, what the symptoms are and how practitioners can manage the behaviours exhibited by this disorder.

_____

_____

_____

_____

_____

_____

_____

_____

_____

_____

Compare your thinking with the information provided below – does the discussion support or challenge your thinking?

Children with autism are usually characterized by three different types of disability:

1. a rigidity of thought and behaviour,
2. limited/impaired verbal and non-verbal communication and
3. difficulty with social relationships and interactions.

A useful summary by Wing (1988) explores these disabilities through the 'Triad of Social Impairments' as detailed below:

◆ social understanding and imagination;
◆ social communication;
◆ social recognition.

Dealing with the facts

◆ Autism is a common developmental disorder.
◆ Autism affects all races, ethnic groups and socio-economic backgrounds.
◆ Boys are three to four times more likely than girls to have autism.
◆ There is no cure for autism.
◆ Autistic children will exhibit a wide range of symptoms with varying levels of severity – some children will require lifelong care and supervision while others will be able to live independent lives.

Recognizing these symptoms will allow a practitioner to make more of an informed opinion about children whom they believe are autistic in their class. These symptoms, guided by nine diagnostic points devised by Creak (1961), include:

◆ Sustained impairment of interpersonal relationships – prefer to be alone.
◆ An unawareness of personal identity.
◆ Preoccupation with particular objects – fascination with repetitive movements.
◆ Striving to maintain 'sameness' – routine, routine, routine!
◆ Acute anxiety produced by change – inability to cope.
◆ Abnormal perceptual experience (hearing and vision).

◆ Failure to develop speech beyond a very limited level – abnormal in content and quality.
◆ Distortion of movement.
◆ Some learning difficulties, but some evidence of particular skills or abilities or knowledge.

(Cited in www.mugsy.org/connor2.htm)

 Think about your class!

Take a moment to reflect on the points highlighted above:

◆ Do any of these mirror the behaviours of children in your class?
◆ Are their behaviours of concern to you?
◆ How do other children in your class react/engage with these children?

While there is no known cure for autism there is also no known certainty as to what causes it in children, although reviews of studies suggest the effects of a variety of conditions including rubella, whooping cough, allergies, measles or a lack of oxygen at birth could adversely affect a child's developing nervous system. Emotional trauma (bad parenting) and vaccinations are *no longer* accepted as potential causes.

Children who appear distant, do not play or interact well with others, are uncommunicative, have problems speaking, have uncontrollable temper tantrums, find eye and physical contact difficult, insist on sameness and routine, and engage in repetitive or compulsive actions will present behavioural difficulties for practitioners to deal with. Effective intervention and management are essential if we are to ensure these children continue to be well-integrated into mainstream situations.

What to avoid

Make a list of approaches you would avoid using to manage the behaviours of children with autistic tendencies. Compare these to the strategies suggested below as good practice – are there any direct comparisons?

_____

_____

_____

_____

_____

_____

◆ Provide a clear structure to the day with a set daily routine.
◆ Use clear and unambiguous language.
◆ Set clear expectations for behaviour – avoid lowering your standards.
◆ Appreciate autistic children will have 'bad days'.
◆ Address the child individually.
◆ Provide plenty of warning for changes in routine/activities.
◆ Make instructions and requests simple.
◆ Use visual cues and signals.
◆ Always check understanding by repeating/rephrasing sentences.
◆ Differentiate tasks to ensure children can access them at their level of attainment.
◆ Teach explicit social skills.
◆ Remove/minimize distractions as and when necessary.
◆ Use other practitioners to support children in eliminating stress.
◆ Use various teaching tools – ICT, music, drama – to engage learners.
◆ Maintain a dialogue with parents and carers.
◆ Seek specialist support in diagnosis and strategies/intervention programmes.
◆ Speak to the SEN co-ordinator for guidance and advice.

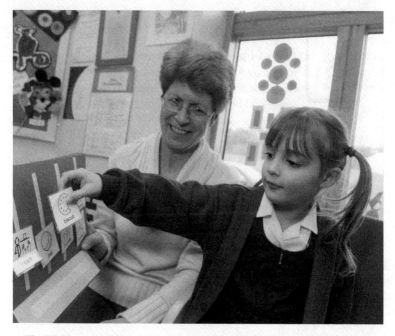

The PECS approach (Picture Exchange Communication System) is an effective way to support children with autistic tendencies in terms of helping them to structure their working day in school. For more details see www.pecs.org.uk

References

Creak, M. (1961) 'Schizophrenic Syndrome in Childhood', *Cerebral Palsy Bulletin* 3, pp. 501–4.

Wing, L. (1998) 'The Continuum of Autistic Characteristics', in B. Schopler and N. Mesibov (eds), *Diagnosis and Assessment in Autism*, New York: Plenum Press.

69. Supporting gifted children in the classroom

I have just started a job share in a Year 3 class and one child stands out from the rest in terms of academic test results. While I am trying to cater for this child's academic needs in each lesson, I am aware that his personal and social capabilities are somewhat lacking and this is having an effect on his ability to make and keep friends in class. What can I do to support him?

Year 3 class teacher, job share

Being a gifted pupil in school means that, like everyone else in the class, he has a range of needs which must be met by a devised programme of appropriate provision to ensure the child achieves his full potential.

Remember, oh do remember

Gifted pupils need to engage in provision which caters for their overall holistic development. Work should be balanced to support a child's academic, personal, social and emotional development.

Being gifted does not necessarily mean that a child is able to succeed in tests or examinations. The term 'gifted' means much than this and takes into consideration children's possible leadership qualities, practical skills and a capacity for creative thought. Children who are musical or who excel in sports or areas including dance and art and design are also considered to be gifted.

Top Tip!

Practitioners should ensure they carefully read the school's policy on gifted pupils so that they are clear as to what the school considers to be 'gifted'.

If asked, many practitioners would identify children who are of low ability who would cause behavioural issues in the classroom. However, if the needs of gifted pupils are not met through careful planning and teaching, these children are likely to:

◆ sigh/yawn heavily if work is not pitched at the right level for them;
◆ not listen to the practitioner if subject matter does not stimulate them;
◆ rush work if tasks do not provide any sort of challenge for them;
◆ become increasingly restless if questions asked by the practitioner fail to develop their level of thinking;

◆ behave inappropriately to relieve levels of boredom they have to endure as a result of unstimulating or unchallenging homework.

> **Reflection Time!**
> ◆ Do you have any gifted children in your class?
> ◆ How do you know?
> ◆ What procedures do you have in place to assess whether a child is gifted in your school?
> ◆ How do you cater for their needs in taught sessions?
> ◆ How involved are parents/carers in supporting provision in the classroom/at home?

Children from the ages of three upwards can be referred to as 'gifted' and it does not matter if you are male or female or are of a particular ethnic background: all children are potentially gifted. Schools should therefore ensure they have effective identification procedures in place which accurately record criteria and sources of evidence, and regularly monitor progress and assessment data throughout the school year.

To support gifted pupils emotionally practitioners should use lots of PSHCE and circle time opportunities, getting them to work with different children to help form relationships. In relation to a child's academic development there are three main ways curriculum provision can be made. Please see the Which is which? task opposite.

Provision for gifted pupils can also be made through the following:

◆ Differentiation strategies, e.g. breadth, depth and pace of taught delivery.
◆ Groupings the children work in.
◆ Use of new technologies to promote personalized learning.
◆ Extra-curricular activities with which the children are able to engage.
◆ Attending gifted summer schools.

Which is which?

ENRICHMENT EXTENSION ACCELERATION

Take a look at the detail provided in the table below and decide where each of the words above fit into the second column.

No.	Type of provision	Strategies for provision
1		◆ Child is moved to work with older children. ◆ Work of older children is used in a class for younger children.
2		◆ Children are encouraged to use their higher order thinking skills, e.g. Bloom's taxonomy (1956). ◆ Children to engage in more independent and self-directed learning.
3		◆ Additional resources. ◆ New learning opportunities, e.g. an open-ended project. ◆ Spending longer on extended pieces of work.

Please see below for the answers

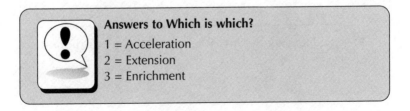

Answers to Which is which?

1 = Acceleration
2 = Extension
3 = Enrichment

70. Children with Tourette's Syndrome

I have just recently had a new little boy start in my class and his behaviour has sparked a lot of interest and comments with the rest of the children. He has what I can only describe as 'tics' – sudden movements of the body (hands/arms) which are repeated over and over again for no apparent reason at all. How can I support this child as I am quite worried about him?

Year 2 teacher

Terminology clarification

Tourette's Syndrome is also referred to as Tourette Syndrome, Tourette's, TS and sometimes Tourette Spectrum Disorder. For the purposes of this section we will refer to it as Tourette's Syndrome.

Test Yourself!

Answer the following questions and then compare your responses to the information and suggestions made in this section – please do not cheat!

◆ What is Tourette's Syndrome?

_____

_____

_____

_____

◆ In whom is it common – boys or girls?

_____

◆ Can Tourette's Syndrome be cured? Yes or No? (Please circle)

◆ What behaviours might sufferers exhibit? List at least four different behaviours:

_____

_____

_____

_____

◆ How can practitioners manage these behaviours in the classroom?

_____

_____

_____

_____

Tourette's Syndrome is an inherited neurological disorder character-ized by involuntary body movements and uncontrollable vocaliza-tions known as 'tics'. These may be combined with sudden outbursts of swearing and other obscenities (referred to as coprolalia) which is a very uncommon symptom, albeit a highly publicized feature of the disorder.

Important to remember!
Children may only be diagnosed as having Tourette's Syndrome if they have suffered with these tics for at least 12 months. This is because it is common for children (approximately 10 per cent) to suffer from brief periods or one-off episodes of tics and for them to make a full recovery.

Tourette's tics usually begin between the ages of five and seven, peaking at around ten years old. During the child's adolescent years and up to the age of 18 tics may begin to diminish. Some children, however, will have their tics for life which may even become even more severe in adulthood. This condition is more likely to develop in boys than in girls.

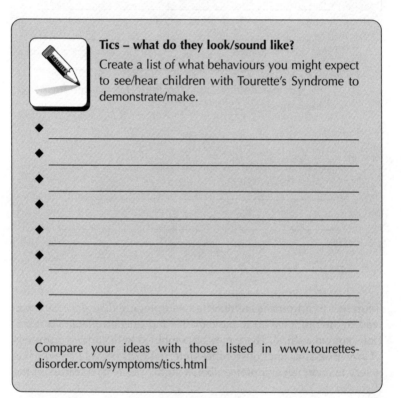

Tics – what do they look/sound like?

Create a list of what behaviours you might expect to see/hear children with Tourette's Syndrome to demonstrate/make.

◆ _____

◆ _____

◆ _____

◆ _____

◆ _____

◆ _____

◆ _____

◆ _____

Compare your ideas with those listed in www.tourettes-disorder.com/symptoms/tics.html

Here are some key facts practitioners should be aware of before they attempt to manage these behaviours:

◆ There is no known cure.
◆ Symptoms can be treated with various medications, behavioural therapy and alternative treatments although the majority of sufferers do not require any.
◆ Children can sometimes suppress their tics for a short time, yet the effort required to do this is similar to us trying to hold back a sneeze.

◆ Many sufferers have additional problems including OCD, ADD, ADHD, sleep disorders and self-harming behaviours, e.g. lip biting, head banging.

◆ Tics are often worse when a child feels stressed, tired or anxious.

Clearly this disorder has the potential to interfere with learning and teaching if children see one of their peers gyrating uncontrollably or jerking their arm up and down. As this behaviour can happen at any time during the school day children with Tourette's Syndrome may become the butt of children's jokes, be bullied or labelled as some kind of 'freak' unless it is managed effectively.

Positive strategies practitioners may deploy include:

◆ Work with the child in small groups and on a one-to-one where possible.

◆ Try to alleviate stress in the classroom wherever possible – make them aware of time limits and practice fire alarms well in advance.

◆ Play calming music in the background as the children work.

◆ Use practitioner and specialist support to help children in class.

◆ Support the child in making friendships with others in the class.

◆ Use tape recorders and computers to alleviate issues the child has with reading and writing.

◆ Talk to the children in the class – highlight similarities between them and the child with Tourette's Syndrome. Stress any differences make people unique.

◆ Work closely with the parents and carers, sharing and adopting good practice though a professional dialogue – oral and/or written.

◆ Avoid drawing attention to the child's tics as you teach. Discourage children in the class from doing this as well.

◆ Praise the child as and when appropriate to maintain and raise his self-esteem.

71. Children with ADHD

There is one child in my nursery group who I really worry about. He is easily distracted, unable to follow instructions, forgetful and never seems to be listening to anything said to him. He is very impulsive – I found him up the tree in the outdoor play area and when I asked him why he had climbed it he said he 'just wanted to'! What can I do to manage this testing behaviour?

Early Years practitioner

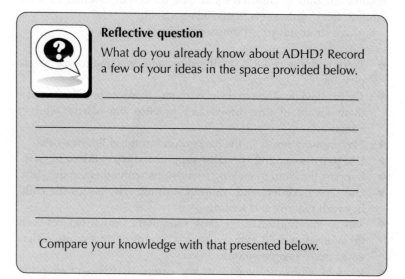

Reflective question

What do you already know about ADHD? Record a few of your ideas in the space provided below.

_____

_____

_____

_____

_____

Compare your knowledge with that presented below.

Attention Deficit Hyperactivity Disorder (ADHD) is potentially a worrying blend of children being impulsive, lacking in inhibition and concentration, having no sense of danger and/or poor social skills, and an inability to respond to the word 'no'. There are a number of warning signs for recognizing children of all ages with ADHD in addition to those already identified in the quote above:

◆ not paying attention to details;
◆ making careless mistakes;
◆ poor concentration levels;
◆ resisting doing anything which requires thinking or planning;
◆ losing things;
◆ fidgeting and not being able to sit still;
◆ finding it hard to play quietly;

◆ talking excessively;
◆ interrupting and intruding on others' work.

Many children have just a few of these symptoms and thus require a little more support at home and in the classroom, as opposed to having to take medical treatments (stimulant drugs) for children who are real sufferers of the disorder. But, as ever, we cannot really manage the behaviour if we do not know what is causing it.

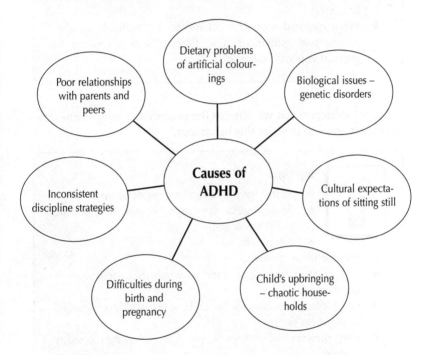

Boys are statistically nine times more likely to have ADHD than girls, but this is not to say that girls do not suffer from it. The effects will vary between the sexes and between each individual child with their need for exercise, their 'short fuse' and low attention span lit by different frustrations.

Find Out!

♦ Who in your class/school suffers from ADHD? How do you know?
♦ What strategies are in place to manage their behaviour?
♦ Which external agencies and support partnerships work with practitioners in your area to manage the children's behaviour?
♦ What national support mechanisms are available to offer advice and guidance? (Use internet search engines to support you with this.)

So, what strategies can we offer to the practitioner who seems desperate for ways to manage this behaviour?

Top Tips!

♦ Avoid having unrealistic expectations.
♦ Make regular eye contact – seek this from the children as well.
♦ Keep calm.
♦ Provide clear routines.
♦ Use plenty of praise specific to when their behaviour is good.
♦ Provide opportunities for the child to go outside and run off some of his energy.
♦ Keep options and choices simple – avoid having too many of them.
♦ Stay on the child's side – it is not her fault!
♦ Be consistent.

It is important for practitioners to not only manage the child's behaviour but also their own – dealing with children with ADHD can be frustrating and physically/emotionally draining.

♦ Do talk to other practitioners about how you are feeling.
♦ Keep in regular contact with parents of children with ADHD – they will be most probably going through the same sort of thing

as you. Plan frequent meetings, use a daily log or make phone calls.
◆ Do not take your anger and frustration out on the child.
◆ Cry/scream/stamp your feet/shout at the *end* of the day!
◆ Use vigorous physical exercise to release frustrations.
◆ Avoid using alcohol to cope with ADHD (you, not the child!).

While the strategies provided above are not exhaustive they do offer a firm base of good practice for practitioners struggling to manage this behaviour. There are, however, other suggestions which may be beneficial to use:

◆ Seek the support of local GPs – ask for leaflets and ask questions.
◆ Talk to the school cooks about the content of foods served to the children.
◆ Provide fast-paced computer games to reward good behaviour.
◆ Use time out if you need to – this is a good strategy for you and the child!
◆ Distract the child with a stimulating activity if his behaviour is upsetting others.
◆ Plan for one-to-one during lessons/sessions so needs are suitably met.

A useful book to support knowledge, understanding and ideas relating to this behaviour is: Livingstone, T. (2005) *Child of Our Time*, London: Bantam Press, esp. pp. 293–5.

72. Managing children with physical impairments

I have been informed by the headteacher that I will have a new child joining my class in the spring who is physically impaired. I have no idea what that actually means nor do I know what implications this will have for my practice in the classroom – will they 'play' on their disability? What can I do?
Year 4 teacher

The first thing to do is not panic! Most practitioners experience some form of anxiousness when they are made aware of children coming into their class who have some kind of physical disability. It is only when they undertake some background research (never make any assumptions until you have all the facts), and meet the child and their parents/carers that practitioners realize that a number of common sense changes need to be made to integrate them successfully into the classroom environment.

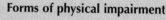

Forms of physical impairment

There is a wide range of physical impairments and children cover the whole ability range. Using the internet identify six different types of physical impairment and record what strategies practitioners could put in place to support these children if required:

Impairment	Strategies for support
Wheelchair bound	Extensions on table legs to bring them to appropriate height, rearrange furniture to allow easy access.

Make a note of the best websites you visited and share these with your colleagues.

_____

_____

_____

_____

_____

_____

_____

It is important to realize that it is not possible to generalize about children with physical differences – a child may have cerebral palsy or be born with no fingers on one hand, yet may be able to access the curriculum and learn effectively without additional educational provision. However, there are a number of medical conditions associated with physical disabilities which may impact on mobility. These include:

♦   heart disease;
♦   muscular dystrophy;
♦   spine bifida;
♦   hydrocephalus.

With children also suffering from sensory impairments, neurological problems and learning difficulties, practitioners must ensure they become as knowledgeable as they can about the child and his or her disability.

This 'knowledge' . . . how do I acquire it?

Take a moment to consider a) ways in which practitioners can gather information and b) to whom
they can speak/consult to aid their understanding
of the child and their disability. Use the chart
below to record your ideas.

Ways	People
◆ Academic texts ◆ Research	◆ The children themselves ◆ The child's parents/carers

Encourage one of your colleagues to complete a blank copy of
the grid and compare ideas – does their chart support or
extend your thinking in any way?

As this book does not claim to be an expert source of information on
all issues relating to Special Education Needs, practitioners are
encouraged to download information from the internet relating to
physical impairment to develop their knowledge, skills and understanding.

Irrespective of the age or gender of the child, behavioural issues are certain to develop if the child's needs are not catered for. These are not solely educationally based – environmental, emotional, social and physical needs are factors to be considered as well. Behaviours explored in this book could easily be demonstrated by children with physical impairments and reasoning behind the use of these is likely to be very similar. Management strategies for these specific behaviours may need to be adapted slightly, yet your expectations should remain high and be consistent in approach.

The strategies suggested below to include a child with physical impairment would not only benefit all children in your class but would pre-empt any behavioural issues from 'erupting'.

Strategy assessment

Look at the strategies presented below and assess whether A) you use them already, B) you would like to adopt them as your practice or C) whether you do not feel they would work in your setting.

Do ensure:

◆ The physical environment is safe for the child.
◆ Emergency exit plans take into account a child with physical limitations.
◆ Materials are easily accessible and stored for the child to reach, use and return.
◆ You adapt physical activities so children with physical impairments can still be involved.
◆ Work with parents/carers on ways to make things even more accessible.
◆ Game rules are adjusted to accommodate for different needs and abilities.
◆ You encourage children to help those with physical impairments but not to do everything for them.
◆ You maintain and sustain a positive attitude towards the child – pity does not help anyone.

Identify strategies you intend to use by dating them when you intend to review the effectiveness of their integration into your practice.

73. Squash! Squidge! Splat!
Children who deliberately kill living things

I have really taken a dislike to a child who just recently seems to take delight in killing living things. He caught and squashed a butterfly yesterday and is forever stamping on the fresh grass growing on our playing fields. What can I do to make him see that he is being extremely antisocial in his behaviour?

Year 3 teacher

While most children know the difference between right and wrong, some children think that killing living things is acceptable behaviour. Before we explore this behaviour we need to be clear about what we mean by 'living things'. This encompasses a vast number of different types and species of animals and plants, but for the purposes of this section we are focusing on plants, grass, flowers, insects and vegetation.

Take a moment to reflect

- How many children do you know who deliberately kill living things in your class?
- What do they kill?
- Why do they do this?
- How do you manage this behaviour in your class?

Compare responses you make to these questions after reading and reflecting on the information detailed overleaf.

Most children will be unaware that they are being destructive when they engage in activities such as picking daisies to make daisy chains or stepping off the school path onto the surrounding grass. While these appear to be harmless activities children should be made aware of the effect they will eventually have, e.g. no daisies for other children in the school to appreciate and no grass to keep the school grounds looking pleasant.

Top Tips!

◆ Ensure there are child-friendly signs around encouraging children to keep to the paths.
◆ Discourage children from picking flowers – provide them with pencils and paper to draw pictures of them or take digital images.
◆ Conduct lessons which involve living creatures, discussing what they actually do for the environment.

There are, however, children who seem to have a rather destructive streak and get some sort of 'perverse kick' out of pulling plants out of the ground, stamping on flowers and killing worms and bugs that they find. Why do they do this?

◆ Attention seeking, perhaps?
◆ Child does not know *how* to respect living things – has never been taught how or what to do?
◆ Child is young and does not understand his behaviour is wrong?
◆ Child is displeased or angry with herself or others and so takes out her frustration on something which cannot defend itself?
◆ Child is being bullied?
◆ Child is frightened by certain animals – spiders?
◆ Child feels a sense of power in being able to kill if he wants?
◆ Learned behaviour – child has seen peers or siblings doing the same thing?

Whatever the reason practitioners need to put in place strategies to ensure children know that killing living things is unacceptable.

◆ Talk to the child about his behaviour – does *he* think it is acceptable?

- Tell children that their behaviour displeases you.
- Get the child to reflect on the effect this will have on other living things which need particular animals and plants to live.
- Involve the educational psychologist in helping to determine causes and ways to help the child.
- Closely monitor the child's behaviour when she is outside.
- Use time out to give children a chance to reflect on their actions.
- Remove privileges or issue additional homework as a punishment for their actions.

Practitioners can implement a number of strategies to prevent issues of this nature from arising. See the suggestions box below for potential ideas.

Suggestions Box

Children will learn more about the importance of looking after living things if they are actively involved in doing this. Engage the children in any of the following:

- Reading/talking about books linked to looking after animals and plants.
- Encourage outside speakers to come in and talk about caring for animals and plants.
- Grow various plants inside and outside the classroom – give different children opportunities to water them.
- Have a class pet which can be taken home at the weekends.
- Have a school garden which children can visit and tend.
- Run science, gardening, environmental and animal welfare after-school clubs.
- Set up a local environmental role play area inside the classroom.

Consider which strategies you would like to integrate into your practice. Review the progress you and your children make a couple of weeks after implementing these strategies – how effective have they been?

74. Ag . . . gres . . . SION! The 'aggressive' child

One boy in my class is just so aggressive! One minute he is all calm and doing his work, and then something happens and he becomes the Incredible Hulk *– all raging and 'Raaaaa'! His carers have the same problems with him at home. Why is he like this and how can I help him to control this aggression?*

Year 3 Teaching Assistant

Most practitioners regard aggression in children as 'undesirable' or 'harmful', particularly as incidences they remember in the classroom may have resulted in tears, physical harm or even bloodshed (a bleeding nose!). While it is difficult to define aggression there are generally two recognized types of aggression:

Type	Gender	Characteristics	Reasoning
Physical	Boys	Kicking, biting, punching others	Higher levels of testosterone in their bodies, developed physical strength in older males
Verbal	Girls	Gossiping, writing unkind notes, spreading false stories, pinching	Linguistic capabilities develop more quickly and effectively in females

It is important to remember though that there will be girls who are more physically aggressive in nature, and boys whose language will be sufficient enough to verbally harm others – there will always be children who don't fit the norm!

While a rather negative viewpoint is presented aggression is actually a natural driving force which is designed to give us energy and enterprise. As an integral part of the human makeup some see aggression as a favourable necessity yet, whatever your view, it is clear aggression has the potential to upset and hurt others. So why is it used?

A moment for critical reflection

Select one child you work with in your class who demonstrates aggressive tendencies. Consider why she uses aggression and when it is used.

Make a note of your ideas and compare them to the rest of this section.

Children will become aggressive mainly out of frustration as a result of the following situations:

- They want your attention and cannot get it.
- They are uncomfortable.
- They want to play with a toy which is being used by another child.
- Something is unfair or out of bounds.
- They are unable to be first in the line.

Aggressive tendencies can occur at any time during the day yet are dependent on a range of factors which may influence the use of it. These include:

◆ Poor social and/or communication skills.
◆ Tiredness and exhaustion.
◆ Competition or rivalry.
◆ Home influences – culture, religious, parental expectations, socio-economic.
◆ Media influences – film, radio, TV, music, computer games, and internet images.
◆ Poorly behaved role models – children, parents, carers and practitioners.
◆ Reactions to change – smells, temperature, noise levels, amount of space available, the weather.
◆ Traumatic family incidences – bereavement, serious illness, abuse, divorce or separation.
◆ Stage of child development – age, sex, maturity, concentration levels, attention span.
◆ Personality clashes with practitioners and peers.
◆ Attention seeking.
◆ Hunger – drop in blood sugar levels.

Top Tips!

There are a number of top tips you can use to effectively manage aggression:

◆ When attracting the attention of the child, lower your voice and talk quietly, using clear and concise language to instruct him.
◆ Avoid arguing with the child as this will only aggravate the situation.
◆ If the child is a potential danger to herself or others, physically restrain her.
◆ Remind the child of the rules of the classroom.
◆ Use time out systems to give the child an opportunity to calm down.
◆ Give the child two choices, e.g. 'Either chose a different toy to play with or sit with me for five minutes!' Most children usually go for the easiest/nicest option!
◆ Try to channel the child's aggression into a purposeful physical activity – running races, football, playing on the bikes.
◆ Remember that it is the behaviour you are unhappy about, not the child.

Reflection on current practice

Take a moment to reflect on the tips identified above – which of these do you already use? Which tips do you try to use but which do not seem to work for you? Which tips will you adopt to improve your practice?

Indicate these tips on the list above by using the letters **U** for those which you use, **D** for those which do not seem to work for you and **A** for those which you would like to adopt.

Set yourself a review date by when you will reflect on the use and effectiveness of these tips using the support space provided:

Date of review: _____

Notes on effectiveness of tips:

_____

_____

_____

_____

New tips to try:

_____

_____

_____

_____

Date for review of new tips: _____

75. Feeling low: Children suffering from depression

When I think of my class I see smiling faces and bright eyes – they are happy and seem to really enjoy being at school. There is, however, one child who seems to be . . . well . . . the only word I can use to describe it is 'depressed'. I know adults suffer from it but the behaviours he exhibits really seem like depression to me – am I right to say this? What can I do to help this child?

Year 3 teacher

Fact: Adults are not the only ones to get depressed. Children and teenagers can also suffer from depression, yet it is difficult to be certain whether they are 'just going through a phase' or really are depressed.

What do you already know?

To assess the value of this section make a note of all of the things you know about depression in the space below.

_____

_____

_____

_____

_____

_____

_____

While reading the rest of this section put a number **1** against anything you already knew and a **2** against anything which helps to move your knowledge, skills and understanding forwards.

It is important to realize that depression is actually an illness and can get much worse if it is not treated. It can prevent children from enjoying their formative years and those children (particularly teenagers) who suffer from it are at risk of potentially committing suicide. While depression is more common in older children, children of all ages are prone to suffering from it, irrespective of whether they are male or female. But how do we know if a child is depressed or not?

Depressed or not?
Put a tick or a cross against the behaviours listed below which you feel indicate whether a child is depressed or not.

◆ Slow thinking [   ]
◆ Loss of energy – tired [   ]
◆ Restless [   ]
◆ Anxious [   ]
◆ Fear of school [   ]
◆ Dislike of being away from parents/carers [   ]
◆ Stop talking to friends and family members [   ]
◆ Being or feeling sad [   ]
◆ Irritable [   ]
◆ Unable to concentrate or make decisions [   ]
◆ Loss of interest in friends and activities [   ]
◆ Loss of appetite or eating too much [   ]
◆ Harms themselves [   ]

For the answers please refer to the end of this section.

Children do not need to have all the symptoms presented above to be depressed. However, if they are sad and irritable for most of the day, and have lost interest in their friends and activities they once used to enjoy, then clearly something is wrong. As opposed to voicing their feelings of sadness like adults, children are more prone to be grumpy or cry. They may say they have headaches or stomach pains.

Clearly depression can have an adverse effect on children's schoolwork, their relationships with family, friends and practitioners, and their ability to cope with life in general. But to effectively help children with depression we need to be clear on what causes depression. Interestingly no one knows for sure what causes it but a combination of the following are more likely to bring about depression in children:

♦ Something bad in their life is happening, e.g. death in the family, abuse, separation or divorce, being bullied at school, illness.
♦ Onset of puberty.
♦ Changes in how the brain works – chemical imbalance.
♦ History of depression in the family.

Children who are depressed may need to be convinced that they are ill and need help. Ways in which practitioners can help these children include:

♦ Keeping up to date with issues surrounding the child's life.
♦ Talking to the child about her feelings and the feelings of others.
♦ Being available to listen to them when they want to talk to you.
♦ Helping children to remember the good times.
♦ Using praise to lift their spirits.
♦ Making the child an integral part the classroom.

Depression can be treated. With this in mind practitioners should consult with parents/carers, education psychologists, Local Authorities and local GPs for information and strategies for support. Talking treatments (known as psychotherapy) can help mild symptoms of depression whereas treatment with drugs called antidepressants can help with severe depression although there is a serious risk of side effects.

Answers to Depressed or not?

All the behaviours indicate some degree of depression. There are more symptoms practitioners should be aware of. You are encouraged to read the information contained in the following website:

http://www.rcpsych.ac.uk/mentalhealthinformation/mental-healthandgrowingup/34.depressioninchildren.aspx

76. Drink and drugs: Children who bring inappropriate items into school

Last week I found a packet of tablets in the hands of a boy in my class. The day before we had an incident with a girl who had brought miniature bottles of whiskey in to share with her nine-year-old friends! What can I do to make these children see that this is a very worrying issue in our class and for our school as a whole?

Year 5 teacher

Children who bring different forms of drugs and alcoholic drinks on to the school premises pose a real issue for practitioners because the misuse and consumption of these could be potentially fatal. It is important for children of all ages to understand that this behaviour is very serious indeed.

Reflective questions

◆ What kinds of drugs/drink do children bring into your school?
◆ From where do the children get them?
◆ From whom do the children get them?
◆ Why do children bring these items into school?
◆ How do children get them into school?

Discuss your ideas with other colleagues.

One of the first things we must do is clarify what is meant by the terms 'drink' and 'drugs'.

What does it mean to you?
Create a list of your thoughts and ideas relating to the question below:

Q: What does 'drink' and 'drugs' mean to you?

_____

_____

_____

_____

_____

Take a few moments to glance through the following websites which will provide you with further ideas and clarify thinking:

http://www.kidshealth.org/kid/grow/drugs_alcohol/know_drugs.html
http://www.kidshealth.org/parent/positive/talk/talk_about_drugs.html

With any behaviour, there are always reasons as to why this happens in school, and this behaviour is no exception. Possible reasons include the child:

◆ has been 'dared' to smuggle items into school by peers or siblings;
◆ thinks it is 'big' to have items of this nature about his person;
◆ thinks it is a game – 'some sort of counters from a board game?';
◆ is going through an 'experimentation stage' – cigarettes and alcohol;
◆ is curious – what do they do? How do they affect you?
◆ is trying to act grown up;
◆ is seeking attention;
◆ thinks items are 'sweets' and 'fizzy drinks';
◆ thinks it is okay as these items are at home – parents have them lying around the place.

Scenario

During 'Show and Tell' a child proudly produces a packet of cigarettes belonging to her mother to show the rest of the class. What would you do?

Consider the value of the strategies below to support your practice.

If you do find drink or drugs on children ensure you avoid:

◆ confronting them in front of their peers;
◆ overreacting;
◆ blaming yourself – it is not your fault;
◆ shouting at the child;
◆ lecturing the child;
◆ consuming them yourself at the end of the day (even if your day gets worse!).

Instead practitioners are recommended to:

◆ calmly speak to the child in a quiet voice;
◆ speak to the child on a one-to-one;
◆ speak to the whole class about the dangers of drink and drugs if they see them being handled by a child;
◆ ask the child why he has them, where he got them and whom they are for;
◆ firmly ask the child to hand over the items;
◆ ensure they are locked securely away;
◆ make a written log of what happened and when;
◆ speak to your headteacher, the child protection officer and the police;
◆ inform parents and carers.

Important considerations:

Some children have to have certain drugs about their person – creams, Epi pens, inhalers. These should be clearly labelled with the child's name and stored safely.

Virtually all parents/carers will be deeply distressed by their child's behaviour yet they need to consider what they can do at home to prevent it happening again. Parents/carers should be advised to ensure that drink and drugs of any kind should be:

◆ out of children's reach;
◆ stored in a high cupboard;
◆ locked away;
◆ stored in child-proof bottles.

Schools should ensure they have effective preventative measures in place to ensure this kind of behaviour does not become a regular occurrence. Possible strategies include using:

◆ PSHCE and circle time opportunities – 'good' and 'bad' medicines;
◆ learning and teaching time during science and PE lessons;
◆ the local constabulary and the school nurse for 'talks';
◆ local and national drug awareness schemes of work;
◆ videos, pamphlets and books;
◆ role play and drama.

77. Knives, guns and machetes: Weapons found on children in school

My class was having a great afternoon doing some art work when one of the children accidentally spilt some water over another child's painting. The child jumped up, raced to his drawer and pulled out a hammer which he threatened to 'smash' the other child's 'brains out' if she was not more careful! It was the most frightening experience of my life! What can I do to prevent scenes like this happening again?

Year 5 teacher

The number of children bringing weapons into school is on the increase and of regular national headline news. As current research identifies children as young as four years old having weapons found about their person in schools, it is clear that a 'War on the Weapons' needs to be conducted to combat the issues surrounding this worrying recent development in children's behaviour.

Reflective questions

◆ Do children in your school bring weapons with them to class?

◆ If so, why do they do this?

◆ Do you know from where they get these weapons?

◆ What short-term strategies do you put in place when you find a child who has a weapon?

◆ Who do you involve in helping you manage this behaviour?

The term 'weapons' encompasses many different implements depending on how they are used, e.g. rulers and pencils. However it is important for practitioners to be aware of the types of weapons children may bring into the classroom and what they actually look like. These include:

◆ knives – lock, pen, flick;
◆ machetes;
◆ ball-bearing guns;
◆ knuckle dusters;
◆ screwdrivers;
◆ hammers;
◆ baseball bats.

All these weapons could seriously injure and potentially kill if used inappropriately, and children need to be educated so that they fully understand and appreciate the risks involved in carrying and using weapons.

Top Tip!

Involve the local police in giving talks to the children about the dangers of carrying weapons. They should always be involved if a child brings a weapon into school.

It is important for us to address the key question relating to this behaviour – why do children feel the need to carry weapons? Possible reasons include:

◆ curiosity – what does it do?;
◆ a status symbol;
◆ desperation – last resort to stop others hurting them;
◆ a 'substitute' toy;
◆ for protection against bullies;
◆ learned behaviour – child sees parents and siblings using them (but in different contexts, e.g. preparing food, trimming plants);
◆ 'special present' they have which they do not want to lose;
◆ a 'dare' – child has been challenged by peers or siblings to smuggle it into class;
◆ gift for the lead practitioner who needs a sharp knife to open up boxes of resources;
◆ a way to make children 'do things' for them – tool for intimidation and bullying.

Reflection task

Which of the reasons above surprise or shock you? Are there any other reasons why children bring weapons into school?

Most children carry weapons as a result of bullying. Having them close to hand offers a form of protection which compensates for either their lack of physical strength or verbal confidence. However, many children are unaware of the consequences of carrying a weapon, particularly in relation to the law.

The law? What law?

What does the law state about children carrying weapons? Search the internet for websites which provide clear details relating to this. How would you make children aware of these laws in a child-friendly manner?

With weapons making children and practitioners feel unsafe in their working environment, there is a real danger that learning and teaching can be severely disrupted if children threaten or actually use a weapon on another child. If an incident does occur in your class do:

◆ stay calm;
◆ maintain eye contact with the child;
◆ listen to what the child has to say;
◆ speak clearly and calmly;
◆ ask the children nearby to move out of the way;
◆ firmly ask the child to put the weapon on the floor;
◆ empathize with the child's feelings yet make it clear that her behaviour is unacceptable;
◆ use physical force if/where appropriate or necessary.

Schools need to ensure they have procedures in place to help children who bring in weapons and those emotionally distressed by incidents involving weapons. Policies and practice need to be regularly updated with reference to Local Authorities and government recommendations to ensure the most effective approaches are in place to deal with incidents of this nature.

78. *Swish!* Out they go! The child who runs out of class/school

What am I supposed to do when a child runs out of my class? I have one particular child who constantly does it and I am becoming quite distressed by his behaviour. Why is he doing it and what can I do to prevent it from happening?

Reception practitioner

An increasing number of incidents involving children walking out of school have resulted in many settings becoming far more safety conscious to ensure children remain on the premises until the end of the day. The use of high fences, spring-activated doors, electronic keypads, security cameras and 'higher handles' are now standard in most settings to prevent children from wandering out of the school.

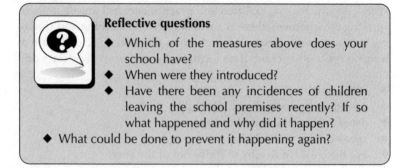

Reflective questions
- ◆ Which of the measures above does your school have?
- ◆ When were they introduced?
- ◆ Have there been any incidences of children leaving the school premises recently? If so what happened and why did it happen?
- ◆ What could be done to prevent it happening again?

Clearly children who go missing can be a 'stomach churning' experience for any practitioner, particularly as they have been entrusted to you by their parents/carers. It is distressing for parents/carers and the child's peers who have temporarily 'lost their friend', and can be an unnecessary strain on police resources used to track the children down. As it is essential to ensure this behaviour is managed effectively, we should consider possible reasons as to why children do it, e.g. the child:

- ◆ may see it as a 'game' of hide and seek;
- ◆ likes the attention it brings;
- ◆ is more interested in what is happening outside;
- ◆ finds the work set too difficult or unstimulating;
- ◆ has been challenged by a peer or sibling to 'bolt the gates';
- ◆ has learned how to open the doors;
- ◆ does not like being confined into a particular space;
- ◆ is curious of surroundings and wants to explore;
- ◆ dislikes school and wishes to be home;
- ◆ practitioners have not properly secured the environment before the children use it.

There are many times during the school day during which children can 'escape', so it is important that all adults working in the setting are aware of these times and what measures need to be in place to prevent an incident occurring.

Find Out!
Work with a colleague and individually make a list of all of the times when a child could 'slip through the school net' during a typical school day. Consider what measures are in place to prevent this from happening and who is responsible for ensuring these measures are in place. Compare your lists.

While we have already highlighted strategies to improve school security these are costly and affect school and LA budgets. Although necessary, there are other strategies settings can use to prevent this behaviour from occurring:

◆ Take children on a trip around the local area so their curiosity is satisfied.
◆ Plan engaging activities in the classroom.
◆ Ensure doors are properly closed and securely locked before teaching commences.
◆ Plan for adult supervision to be available during key times during the day when children may run out of school.
◆ Use adult support to closely monitor the behaviour of 'bolters'. Make them aware of potential warning signs.

Controversial Case Study
A headteacher, so concerned about the possibility of children wandering out of his school, decided to adopt a 'shock tactic' approach. During one assembly he told the school the story of a child who walked out of school and was never seen again. Using digital images (of his son) the headteacher discussed the motives of the child and how the boy's parents, teachers and friends felt when the boy never returned. Once he had finished the headteacher scanned the hall – many of the infants had tears in their eyes and the juniors were certainly subdued.
The story was fictitious.
To date no children have been reported leaving the school premises without adult consent or supervision.

Clearly this approach would not suit every practitioner yet there are a number of other ways settings can stop children wandering:

◆ Make children clearly aware of potential dangers outside school.
◆ Use stories, songs, images and videos.
◆ Invite the police to speak to the children about keeping safe.
◆ Work with parents/carers to manage behaviour consistently.
◆ Use PSHCE and circle time opportunities to discuss rules and expectations.
◆ Make 'counting heads' an integral part of your daily practice!

79. *Both* hands on top of the table!
Children who masturbate in school

We have a vet's role-play area and it has proved to be, in some cases, very popular. I 'visited' it one afternoon and was shocked to see a little girl 'bouncing up and down' on one of the soft toys – it soon became apparent that she was pleasuring herself. I could not believe it! What should I have done as I do not think I handled the situation particularly well?

Year 2 teacher

While many practitioners reading this will either have a private giggle or become a little uncomfortable and 'hot under the collar', it is essential that you understand that masturbation in young children is extremely common and should be considered a normal behaviour – even though practitioners and parents may (and probably will) be embarrassed by it.

Reflective questions
◆ How often do you see or have you caught children in your class masturbating?
◆ Do you find that more boys are prone to 'play' with themselves or more girls? Why do you think this is the case?
◆ What do you do when you find a child masturbating? How do you react?

The way a practitioner reacts to finding a child either with their hands in their underwear or rubbing themselves up against other children or objects (for example a radiator) has a direct impact as to how well the behaviour is managed.

Scenario

Imagine you walk into your classroom to find one of your children 'stimulating' themselves. Would you:

a) overreact (shout, scream, and cry)?
b) underreact (roll your eyes, smile)?
c) do nothing (carry on as normal)?

Make a note of why you would react in this way.

Clearly none of the responses above are helpful; practitioners need to be confident about acting in a way which is supported by your whole school approach to

a) behaviour management
b) sex education.

While schools should have up to date policies relating to these key areas, they should ensure their behaviour policy takes into consideration aspects of the sex education policy as some sexual behaviour is normal/acceptable as part of developing social relationships, e.g. touching each other, holding hands, hugging, kissing.

Children's sexual development progresses through a series of stages which, in boys particularly, begins right from birth. Practitioners should be aware of this and are therefore recommended to view the content of the following website: http://www.med.umich.edu/1libr/yourchild/masturb.htm.

Important!

Children's curiosity fuels much of their interest in matters of a sexual nature. They have a natural desire to learn about their bodies, their emotions and those of others. Sexual behaviour between children in school is normal. It is important, therefore, not to think of all sexual behaviour as a sign of abuse.

While most sexual behaviour in children is accidental, experimental or undertaken on a voluntary basis, the behaviour of some children may be the result of being overexposed to adult sexual material or to abuse of a physical, emotional or sexual nature. These children will either be very secretive about their 'activities', very reactive or may abuse other children. In these situations schools should seek the support of specialist help so that a 'whole child' approach can be put in place. These may include:

◆ police;
◆ Parent Teacher Association;
◆ governors;
◆ social services;
◆ behaviour support teams;
◆ educational psychologists;
◆ local authority;
◆ curriculum services – PSHCE / Healthy schools;
◆ health visitor.

To effectively manage this behaviour there are a number of approaches and strategies practitioners can put into place:

◆ Collect information about the child to ascertain whether her behaviour is sexually normal – always make an informed decision.
◆ Don't panic.
◆ Talk to colleagues about behaviours you have seen – are they normal for your school?
◆ Speak to your school's Child Protection Co-ordinator.
◆ Teach the children not to be ashamed of their bodies yet respect that certain parts are private.
◆ Use the correct words for parts of the body.
◆ Provide clear boundaries about what is acceptable in public and private arenas.
◆ Try not to draw too much attention to it.
◆ Redirect the child's behaviour towards something which is more acceptable.
◆ Speak to the group as a whole – allow them to appreciate that it is okay to talk about this behaviour together and with other adults.
◆ Avoid blaming the child – he should not be made to feel guilty about what he has done.

- Don't over-ask questions to obtain excessive detail.
- Keep clear, detailed and factual records about the child's behaviour if this is of a regular occurrence.
- Involve parents and carers.

80. 'I don't know what to do!' When behavioural issues just become too much

There are times when I just don't seem to know what to do about some of the behaviours I have to manage. I just stand there and my mind seems to go blank. I've got to the point where I feel I've tried everything and nothing seems to works. I get a bit depressed because I get so wrapped up in delivering the curriculum that I forget how to manage the children's behaviour and become really irritated by the disturbances they cause. Can you just give me a list of strategies or something?

Year 4 teacher

As this is the final behaviour to be explored in this book then a list is exactly what I'll do!

- Have high expectations of all children irrespective of their age, sex, cultural background or academic ability.
- Be as positive as you can be.
- Have clearly defined classroom rules. Make sure you and the children refer to them regularly.
- Avoid shouting wherever possible.
- Make sure children know it is their *behaviour* which you do not like and not the actual child.
- Use non-verbal positive strategies – a wink, a nod, a smile, a pat on the shoulder, thumbs up.
- Do not lose your temper in front of the children.
- Be clear about what you want and expect from your class and then . . . expect it!
- Ensure children know the consequences of their actions.
- Give children ten times more praise than criticism.
- Change your rewards regularly to stimulate and motivate children.
- Remember that a sticker or a reward given for good behaviour cannot be taken away.
- Stick to any agreements you make with your children.
- Establish the class rules with your class before you attempt to teach them.

- Use behaviour management strategies which promote the use of peer and self-appraisal.
- Say what you mean and mean what you say.
- Never let the children know you are irritated by their behaviour.
- Use a balanced mixture of individual, group and whole-class rewards.
- Please avoid punishing the whole class for one child's behaviour.
- Do not make a big fuss about children's inappropriate behaviour as they will continue to do it.
- Be assertive when you need to be – state what you want and do not back down until you have got it.
- Develop reliable routines in which the children feel warm, secure, welcome and valued.
- Remember that you have the right to teach and the children have a right to learn.
- Ensure you acknowledge good and appropriate behaviours.
- Avoid making children cry on a Friday afternoon – they will not thank you for it!
- Please do not hold a grudge with any child in your class; each day should start afresh.
- Plan for good behaviour every day.
- Avoid being sarcastic – even the most intelligent children will not understand.
- Do not form bad habits, e.g. talking over the children or telling them to 'sssssssshhhhhhhh!'
- Do not use nicknames for the children.
- Please do not leave yourself isolated with an individual child.
- Be very wary of using physical restraint with children.
- Always work to repair and restore relationships.
- Be as fair as you possibly can.
- Build trust and support into your teaching time.
- Do not back off or make bargains with the children.
- Be a role model.
- Identify children who are doing what you want them to do.
- Acknowledge the child's anger.
- Talk to children in a quiet voice when you are unhappy with their behaviour.
- Resolve conflicts calmly and quickly.
- Make sure that the child knows exactly what he has done wrong.
- Take the heat out of the situation as soon as possible – use humour where/if appropriate.
- Ensure the praise you give is genuine.

- Catch children being good.
- Step back if you feel yourself becoming aggravated.
- Plan for safety – either remove the child from the situation, remove her from other children or send for another practitioner for support.
- Link good behaviour to children's identity.
- Smile!
- Always talk to others in a professional manner about children's behaviour in your class and strategies to help manage these.
- Remember that you are not alone – all practitioners have to deal with poor behaviour at one time or another in their careers.

I hope this helps!

Index